# TEN

# DRAGON

# TAILS

# TEN DRAGON TAILS

### BY

### CANDY
### TAYLOR TUTT

## LIBRIS DRACONIS PRESS

Libris Draconis Press
PMB 279, 1296 East Gibson Road, Woodland California 95776
Copyright 2003 by Candy Taylor Tutt

Library of Congress Control Number: 2003090292

ISBN 0-9728124-0-7

*To all those who believe*
*in dragons, and*
*to my family*
*for believing in me~*

# Table of Contents

# <u>LEGACY</u>

She spread out her wings to capture the warmth of early-morning sun. Beside her in the branch-and-rock nest, her two young began to stir and squabble.

~Time for first flight, hatchlings are hungry.~ Effortlessly she took to the air, gliding over cedar-covered slopes and climbing higher to the cooler air currents. Below, roads wound through the mountains, past vineyards and barley fields, to converge on the city that gleamed white as a giant seashell. At its edge lay the ocean, waves glistening, blue as lapis. As she circled above, she was joined by others of her kind, spiraling in the skies, their calls resounding in the clear salt air. Grand, strong and proud as its people, the dragons held dominion over Atlantis.

From below a pinpoint of light flashed, once, then again and again. The female dragon tipped one strong wing and veered down at the dwelling on one of the hills that rose up from the city.

Standing in the open courtyard, the old man squinted up into the bright eastern sky, holding the polished silver plate to reflect the rays back at the dragons that circled overhead. Then he sat down to wait. At last she responded, her tail neatly encircling the fountain as she lowered herself gracefully onto the tiled courtyard. He stepped forward to stroke her long neck.

"Ah, beautiful one, for six weeks now you have not come. But it is summer, and I know you have a new pair of hatchlings." She warbled softly as he scratched her smooth head. "Good, good...more young for the future...we both see to the young, you and I..." He opened a fine cloth pouch that hung from his belt, taking out two perfect seashells and a multicolored glass bead. One front claw gently plucked them from his outstretched palm. He clapped his hands. "Hurry now and there will be treats for your babies!"

The fruit trees lining the terrace swayed in the air as she flapped her wings. Damos watched her graceful form in flight toward the harbor. Though so many years ago, he remembered her first visit clearly. To catch the last bits of meat with a piece of bread, he had tipped up his plate and sunlight had reflected off its polished surface. Curious at the flashing light, a young dragon alighted on the terrace, a female judging by her smallish body and narrow tail. Damos soon found that he could thus attract her, and rewarded her visits with bits of meat and fruit. Then her absence of several weeks provoked disappointment and worry, until one afternoon she flew carefully to the courtyard and proudly set down her first-hatch, a dragonlet, bawling and flapping its fragile wings. Repeated strokings soothed the tiny one, and Damos had looked into the mother's calm green eyes.

"So it is, beautiful one...we guide the young, you and I...it is they who will carry on the legacy of Atlantis."

Damos had served on the Council of Ten, the highest governing authority on Atlantis, among scholars, philosophers and astronomers. He was greatly respected for his vast learning, but moreso for the intuition he commanded, the power to know the future. Damos possessed The Way of Sight.

Over time, families commissioned him to teach their sons, and so it was that for some years three young boys had trudged up the hill carrying tablets and styli for lessons while the dragon swooped and chattered above like an oversize magpie: Kaderis, the older brother, calling out to her, petting her when she lit for a moment; Talan, the younger, ever-turning to look out over the harbor at exotic ships anchored there; and their friend Zerek, ciphering as he walked, eyes fast on his lesson tablet.

Damos often gave small prizes for lessons well learned. To the brothers intent on knowing the ways of the seas, he gave shells found in abundance on the far coast of the island, and to the smaller boy, who quickly mastered mathematics and played at barter, he would award a glass trade bead. The dragon soon learned which boy preferred what trinket, and delivered them when earned, clutched tight in her delicate front claws. The three pupils delighted in her antics, indeed she often proved a distraction from lessons. When, as young men, Talan and Kaderis began to sail, she would often follow them as they departed out to sea, tagging after Kaderis' ship with its billowing wing-like sails.

Damos smiled at his recollection as he prepared a reward for the dragon's errand. He drew great comfort from the splendid winged beasts; throughout his long life, they had nested on the craggy mountain. They were a part of The Way of Order.

Swift and purposeful, the dragon made for the harbor where her sharp eyes found the deep-hulled trading ships of Talan and Kaderis at anchor in the bay, each marked with its own crest, and the wharfside warehouse of Zerek, bustling with merchants and traders.

~Shells for Water-Travelers and bead for Keeper of Goods...They have grown tall and strong...still they return to Old One.~ Her tokens delivered, she ascended for her return to Damos. As she neared the terrace she saw him in the courtyard arranging carved darkwood chairs for his guests.

~Old One moves slowly with all his years, no wings to lift him up.~ She sat on the low wall of the fountain, drinking water that spouted from the sculptured dolphin in its center. Damos approached, carrying a chunk of lamb wrapped in a long grapevine laden with grapes. She grasped the bundle in her small strong jaw.

~Old One kindly feeds us.~ She cooed as he scratched her neck and chin, then raised her wings and flew off.

Shading his eyes with a weathered hand, Damos smiled as he watched her go. A distant rumbling made his smile vanish. No thunderheads in the open blue sky, only a lone dragon circling high over the rock mountain. Reassured by the chatter of birds in the nearby fruit trees, he returned to preparation for his guests. It would, he hoped, take his mind off the runes.

Their ships made fast at anchor, sails furled and cargo unloaded, Talan and Kaderis responded to their summons and hastened through the city to the hillside home of their old teacher. He was always eager to hear of Talan's adventurous voyages, Kaderis' newest ship, and the exotic goods Zerek bought and sold in the marketplace. Houses became fewer and trees lined the road as they left the city. Talan, the taller of the two, looked up and around as they walked.

"I remember how the dragon used to watch us at our lessons," he laughed, teeth flashing white against the black of his beard.

"Yes, and steal my stylus," Kaderis added dryly, looking down at the seashell in his strong hand. "She never stole Zerek's beads."

Talan laughed again. "No one steals Zerek's beads, brother. He is known for his shrewdness all the way to the Inland Sea and beyond."

Kaderis rolled his eyes. "Do not speak of that cursed toad-pond! We fell becalmed there on the last voyage."

"For how long?"

"But one day. Then I gave the order to row." He laughed. "Little brother, you know my oarsmen are well-fed and strong. The ship flew through the water straight as a bird to nest."

"The Greeks power their ships with slaves..." Talan began.

Kaderis made a snort of disgust. "A great nation that still allows the buying and selling of men as though they were beasts. You can be assured that Atlantis will never allow slavery."

"Look! You can see see Damos, waving to us!" Talan

pointed. The brothers sprinted the rest of the way and arrived laughing, out of breath, on the terrace.

A long low bench held a basin and pitcher filled with water, soft folded linen, and olive-balm soap. Jostling with Talan, Kaderis filled the basin with water, washing the dust and ocean-spray salt from his face and neck. Filling a cup with water, he rinsed his mouth and spat over the side of the terrace.

"Well, you've become quite the barbarian," commented Zerek, standing at his side.

Kaderis wiped his face with the linen. "And you've become quite prosperous," he replied, indicating the gold threads that trimmed the edge of Zerek's robe.

"Shall we say, I know how to buy and sell?" Zerek answered smugly.

Kaderis turned his attention to a nearby table, set with wine and cups, bread, cheese and fruit. As he poured wine for himself, Talan held out a cup.

"This is wine, boy, not milk and honey," Kaderis teased, holding the pitcher away.

"A certain woman said that to me on my first voyage," Talan answered, grinning, as he reached up and grasped the pitcher. Then Damos appeared in the doorway of the house, and all three turned respectfully to their teacher.

He came forward and warmly grasped the hands of each in greeting. Kaderis, taller than Damos and stocky, pulled him into a full embrace. "We have truly missed you, Master," he said fondly, releasing the old man with a parting squeeze of his hands.

"My gratitude to you for coming," Damos began, then

gestured. "Please, sit down." Damos seated himself, then paused, rubbing his hands together.

"You summoned us..." Kaderis prompted softly.

"It is the runes. For months now...the first time, I was certain it was a mistake. But then, the same message, over and over..."

The three young men exchanged glances, then Kaderis asked, "What is the message, Master?"

"A great catastrophe is in the future."

All three leaned forward in their chairs and began questioning at once.

"Famine?" Talan asked, followed by Kaderis.

"A great storm?"

"War?" Zerek blurted out, staring at Damos.

The old man held up his hands and shook his head in confusion. The look he gave them was one of despair. "I cannot say. The runes did not..."

"When, then?" Zerek demanded. "A week, a month?"

Damos again shook his head. "That...I do not know..."

Suddenly Talan left his chair and knelt in front of Damos, taking the old man's hand in his. "If you need us, Master, you have only to send word with the dragon. She will find us and we will come to you."

"As quickly as the winds will take us," Kaderis added. He too rose to stand behind Damos' chair, a strong hand on the old man's bony shoulder. Zerek sat frowning, preoccupied, then lifted his cup.

"To Damos," he saluted with a calm smile.

"To Damos," joined Talan and Kaderis.

The old teacher was visibly moved. "Please," he

gestured for them to sit. "Eat, drink, share with me your journeys."

Then, over food and wine, each related their latest adventures. Talan's tale involved a chieftain's daughter, strange food and strong drink, in the cold Tin Isles. Soon all were laughing with him.

"It is curious," he added, "on none of the islands or ports, do I see dragons. Only here. That is how I know I am nearing home, when at last there are dragons in the skies." He leaned back and took a long drink of wine.

"That reminds me- where is our worrisome pet?" asked Zerek, raising an eyebrow.

"Ah, she has a new pair of hatchlings to care for. Perhaps she will join our next gathering," Damos replied, with a thoughtful smile.

Talan turned to his brother. "Does she still follow your ship when you leave the harbor?"

Kaderis nodded. "Yes, like a giant seagull, until we reach the open sea, then she returns home."

"But tell me now, where will your next voyages take you?" Damos asked eagerly.

"Back to the Tin Isles," Talan said, setting his empty wine cup on the table.

Kaderis shook his head. "Warmer waters for me. I will return to trade with the Phoenicians, near Greece."

"I've heard of pirates in those waters..." Talan began.

"Pirates?" Zerek asked sharply.

Kaderis' hand went to the dagger in his belt. "I know of those pirates. We will be ready for them. Do not worry, little brother, I will be at our meeting place in four moons."

"My ship will be waiting at the pillars of Hercules." Talan stood up, squinting into the setting sun.

"You must start back to the city soon," Damos said reluctantly. "At night-"

Kaderis grinned. "I think, Master, after all the years we walked that road as children, we can navigate it even in the dark." He stood, placing a hand on Damos' shoulder. "Please," he said quietly, "send word if you need us. We will come." Damos nodded.

The trio made their farewells and began down the road toward the city. After a short distance, Talan spoke, curious.

"What can the Master's prophesy mean?"

"It means, my friend, that Damos is getting old and his mind is wandering," Zerek answered sarcastically.

"Do not judge so hastily," Kaderis warned. "Damos has The Way of Sight. See to him often, Zerek, and let us know if we need to return."

Zerek sighed, impatient. "Oh, very well."

Suddenly Talan tagged Kaderis' arm and ran past him. "Race you to the bottom, brother!"

"And you will lose!" Kaderis responded, sprinting after him.

Zerek brushed dust from the sleeve of his tunic. "Fools," he muttered.

The hatchlings awakened even before the sun rose, squawking and wiggling nervously.

~The rock mountain rumbles again, far under the earth.~ Their mother nudged them with her snout and twined her tail around them. Once they were calmed, she glided from the nest in the gray morning light, circling the mountains and flying toward the harbor. She passed over a flat rock outcropping where dragons lay to preen and sun themselves; today there were none.

~Fewer dragonkind in skies.~ As she flew lower she saw grasses dried, crops withered. ~Food is scarce~ She neared the hilltops overlooking the city and made for Damos' terrace.

Dust flew as she landed in the courtyard. Damos rushed out to greet her.

"Have you come to see me?" He stroked her neck and face, scratched her small leathery ears .

"I have little food to offer you for your young ones," he said, gesturing to the fruit trees in their pots. Leaves were lackluster and limp, and unripened fruit hung shrunken on brittle limbs.

"What is happening, Beautiful One?" Damos asked sadly as he sank down onto a chair. The dragon gave a soft warble and brushed her jaw against his head. After a time Damos sighed, sat up and placed his palms on his knees.

"I must find something for your brood." He rose from the chair, went into the house, and returned with a loaf of bread.

"It is stuffed with dried figs," he explained, as he handed it up to the female dragon. "Your babies will not go hungry today."

She held the bread firmly in her mouth, ducked her head, then flapped her wings. Tree branches quivered as she soared off the terrace. Damos stood watching her curve round toward her home, then looked down at the city. He placed both hands on the terrace balustrade to keep them from shaking.

That night he dreamed of fire and stone meeting in a great cataclysm, the earth opening to swallow both. He awoke sweating and trembling, and lay in the dark for some time before he slept again. When he awakened it was light out, and he listened for the rumbling until his ears began to hum. Then he realized it was unusually quiet. Damos rose and gathered his robe around him, then as he entered the courtyard, his hands flew to his mouth in horror.

Water no longer spouted from the playful dolphin's mouth. Instead it dripped from a gaping crack in the fountain, spread across broken floor tiles, and trickled down the steps.

He leaned against a column to steady himself, then went back inside and brought out his silver plate. Damos held it aloft and flashed his signal until his old arms ached. At last the dragon dropped from the sky.

"Now...Beautiful One...it is not a game." Unsteady fingers drew a glass bead from the pouch. She grasped it in her strong claws and gazed down at Damos for a moment, then flew straight to the harbor.

Zerek arrived late that day, and appeared immediately relieved.

"Ah yes, Master, what the runes foretold has indeed

come to pass!" he began effusively. "I do not think there is need to summon Talan or Kaderis, do you? I only rejoice that you are safe, and that it is over..."

At this Damos gripped the arms of his chair and stood. "No! It is not over!"

"What? What do you mean?" Zerek stopped in mid-sentence, frowning.

"Have you not noticed, how heat roasts the island like an oven? Have you not heard the rumbling, felt the earth shake?" Damos began to pace, gesturing wildly. "And the dragons- have not dragons circled the skies over Atlantis, every day of your life? Only look, Zerek! How many do you see?" Damos sat down again. "You must do something."

"Do- what can I do?"

"You must go to the Council of Ten. The people must be warned..."

"Warned, of what? You do not know what will occur, or when. What can they do?" Zerek retorted.

"Leave the island."

"Leave?" Zerek put his hands on his hips.

Damos sighed. "A portent of things to come..." he began, his voice faint and tired. "I have seen it again and again in the runes...I cannot say when this...this cataclysm will fall...but if it comes to pass at full harbor, thousands of lives will be lost. "

For a moment Zerek stood silent, frowning, his arms crossed. "Very well," he sighed. "At next Council Meeting, I will..."

Damos began to rise from his chair again. "That will

not be for another moon! It will be too late! You must go to them without delay, it will..."

"Very well, very well," Zerek said abruptly, holding up his hand. "I will go to them in three days. You have my word."

Damos clasped Zerek's hand. "I am grateful to you, Zerek. All Atlantis will..."

"Yes, yes, of course, master," Zerek replied impatiently, pulling away. "I must return to the warehouses now." Nodding at the broken dolphin, he added, " My stonemason will attend to the fountain." Then with a thin, forced smile, he turned and left.

Damos leaned on the terrace and watched him walk down the road. The sky above Atlantis, once blue, was a gray haze that turned the sun orange. High in the distance, one lone dragon circled the city, then flew out to sea and disappeared.

At sunset, the two hatchlings slept, wings folded and tails around each other in a serpentine tangle. Silently she pushed off the ledge and flew to search for food.

~Air is foul~ Quickly she climbed higher with great wingstrokes, into clean, cool air. She soared high above the island, toward the northwest, then flew low, sharp eyes scouting out a meal for her young. Where small ponds and streams had been, cracked earth remained alongside yellow-brown seared plants. The northern hills fared little better, trees silent, abandoned by birds; rivers shrunken and muddy, devoid of fish, no small animals drinking.

~No food.~ She returned to her nest. Awake, in stuffy

darkness, she watched as a dull glow pulsed in the sky over the great mountain.

Damos awoke from fitful sleep. Still groggy, he arose and shuffled out onto the terrace, past the repaired fountain where yellowish, stinking water now dribbled from the mouth of the dolphin. Already the air was dry and hot, the sky a dull gray. Damos yawned, leaned on the ledge and gazed down at the city as his eyes focused. Far below, the harbor was crowded with ships, some still under full sail and many more still anchored. Anger brought him fully awake.

Zerek had not gone to the council!

"I see I have misplaced my trust!" He dressed hastily and started down the road toward the city. It was a long walk in the stifling air, but Damos was fueled by urgency and indignation. Arriving at Zerek's warehouse near the docks, he stepped inside and leaned against a wall to catch his breath. At the far end of the long room, speaking with one of his scribes, stood Zerek.

"Zerek!"

Zerek looked up crossly, then saw his visitor.

"Master, welcome..." he began unctuously.

"You have not done as I asked!" Damos shouted, pointing out at the harbor. "How can you be so blind, do coins in your eyes block out the truth?" The room fell silent. Hastily Zerek made his way across the room.

"Master, come, let me help you. You have had a long journey and I am afraid the heat has affected your mind." Turning, he dismissed the clerks and scribes, then put one arm across Damos' shoulders and steered him into a small room. "Wait here, I will bring us something cold to drink." He patted the old man's back, then left, closing the door behind him.

Perspiring and tired, Damos sank onto a low chair, fuming. The table in front of him was piled with scrolls; idly, he picked one up, unrolled it, and began to read. Then with a gasp, he crumpled the parchment until his knuckles were white. Seconds later the door opened and Zerek entered, carrying a pitcher and cups on a tray.

Damos rose shakily, waving the scroll. "This! This is why you did not go to the council, is it not so? Slaves!" He spat out the words like bitter seeds. "Slave trading on Atlantis! Have you forgotten all I taught you? Have you learned nothing?"

Zerek banged the tray down on the table.

"On the contrary, old man, while those other two dreamers had their heads in the clouds, I learned where the true fortunes are made: in the marketplace!" He spread wide the fingers of one hand and thrust them in Damos' face.

"Five, old man! Five times the profit of a season in the marketplace, I make in one year of slave trading!"

Now quivering with rage, Damos threw down the scroll. "The Council will..."

"The Council be damned!" Zerek screamed. "They will do nothing! And you, you will not tell them!" He grabbed the earthenware pitcher. Water spilled and splashed as he swung it round, then brought it crashing down on Damos' head. The old man slumped to the floor amid shards of broken pottery.

Zerek froze for a moment, and then, quickly gathering up all the scrolls, left the warehouse. Behind him, workers were busy loading and unloading ships along the docks. None noticed the steady white plume puffing from the top of the mountain.

Her young woke before dawn, stirring and squabbling, and she knew the reason: the nest had grown uncomfortably hot. All night in the stifling  darkness she felt the mountain radiate heat. Now it was unbearable.

~ Cannot remain here. Must leave.~ The very idea of departing Atlantis was foreign to her, yet she knew there was no other choice. The urge to stay was strong; here, along with all dragonkind, was her ancestral home. And what of her babies,  still so small? Then she recalled the words of Damos: 'We care for the young, you and I.' Although she had not slept the night, she felt great strength rising inside her. The way was clear.

Carefully she grasped the hatchlings securely in her powerful back claws, then  stretched her wings to their widest and soared down from the rocky crag. With mammoth wingstrokes, she rose higher and higher until she reached the upper altitudes. The air was cold, but it was clear and clean. She headed toward the rising sun, her offspring safely tucked up underneath her belly.

She followed the familiar route until the tall ship was in sight, sails billowing like wings, wings like her own. She circled to slow her descent, landed gently on the stern, then ducked her head and warbled as Kaderis approached her.

The moment he saw her Kaderis was filled with dread: surely she brought the summons from Damos. He rubbed her neck and scratched the fine, feather-like scales around her eyes; then he heard a muffled cheeping, and looked down to see the pair of hatchlings. A cold weight sank like an anchor in his gut; there could be only one reason she had brought him her young.

"It is so, then, Beautiful One. The calamity Damos prophesied has come to pass, a catastrophe so great it has caused you to abandon Atlantis." Tears filled his eyes and he stroked her worn, leathery wings. "Why did he not send for us?" As she leaned down and nuzzled his head with her snout, Kaderis sighed and leaned against her. He knew the answer: there had not been time.

His decksmen clustered nearby and eyed the baby dragons with boyish curiosity. Kaderis straightened, then turned to them.

"Bring food and water for her. Summon the ship's healer, tell him we have two young passengers he must care for."

After eating and drinking, with her young stowed below, the dragon was restlesss. With a wheezy sigh, she unfolded her ragged wings and sat poised on the ship's railing.

"I will guard well the charges you have entrusted to me." Kaderis reached up and patted her neck. "Beautiful One...where will you go?..." Then, his voice catching, he whispered, "May the gods watch over you. Goodbye."

She took flight, dipping so low that she nearly plunged into the sea. With great effort she raised her head, straightened her tail, and rose up into the sky out of sight.

Then realization struck Kaderis, sharp as a dagger point: a disturbance so great on land would surely carry out to sea...

"Bring up the anchor! Oarsmen, to your stations, steersman to the rudder! We make for the open sea! Prepare for storm!"

A short distance away, he heard a young sailor question a decksman. "How can there be a storm? There are no clouds, no wind..."

The answer was good-natured but firm. "Heed well the Master, boy. He knows the moon, the sun, the stars, the wind and the waves."

Head down, Kaderis paused, his strong hands gripping the smooth wooden railing. *Master.* To him Damos was the only one deserving of the title; Damos, who had taught them more than just lessons; Damos, who was gone, as Atlantis was gone, forever.

~Air is clear~ She glided high in the cool sky, eyes failing, flying by instinct, returning to the island for the last time. She saw it from far off: a still, gray line on the horizon. Ugly gray smoke now oozed from the mountain. Going by the few landmarks still visible, she dropped down below the smoke and beheld a scene from the underworld: in the eerie semi-darkness, pieces of ash fluttered like great moths, the harbor was jammed with watercraft, the roads choked with streams of people and animals. Terror, confusion and oppressive heat were everywhere.

~Old One, what of Old One?~ Flying inland from the harbor, she traced the familiar road from the city, up the mountain. Then, as she neared Damos' house, she spied him, limping along with slow uncertainty.

~What has befallen him?~ She flew past once, low, then wheeled around and returned. Damos' tunic was rumpled and dusty, he was missing one sandal, and his face and neck were streaked with dried blood from a gash on his forehead.

~Needs wings to lift him up.~ She seized a firm hold on the back of his tunic. He cried out in fright, then turned, looking up. As he saw her, his eyes widened with amazement.

"Beautiful One! You...you have returned..." He reached up a trembling hand to her, then held tight to one foreleg as her wings propelled them both along.

The road was deserted, leaving no carts or travelers to delay her progress. Every sinew, every muscle, every bone ached, but she was determined to finish this last task. In the courtyard at last, she eased him down onto the tile and lay by his side.

~Old One...I too am old.~ Tenderly she sheltered his bloody head with one of her raw, wind-burned wings and exhaled a long, soft breath.

A great rumbling shook the mountain, its agitations sending boulders down hillsides and shaking buildings from their foundations. The rumbling grew louder still, then with an ear-splitting roar the mountaintop exploded in fire and molten rock. Smoke and ash obscured the sun, and in darkness the island disappeared  into the boiling sea.

Far, far distant, a ship with sails like great dragon wings held its course on the southern trade route. It carried far more than just cargo and crew; secure in its hold was a treasure beyond belief. Two tiny creatures, destined to survive and multiply, would become the  legacy of Atlantis: Dragons, grand, proud and strong.

∧∧∧

# QUETZALCOATL

Deep in his bones, the dragon felt as old and empty as the mountain itself. For ages, legions of men had gouged and carved out prized minerals from its core and stripped the ancient tall trees from its slopes until nothing but rock remained. Snow clung to the northern face of the mountain for much of the year, and food grew scarce in the cold. Crude nomads were the only men that approached.

Lengthening shadows stretched across the entrance of the cave where, unseen, the dragon listened to the men below as they made their clumsy ascent. Soon it would be dark; perhaps the intruders would be satisfied to merely scale the hillside and depart. He sighed a rumbling hiss.

Suddenly they streamed into the cave, brandishing weapons by torchlight. He felt a quick sting in his side; a torch burned the tip of his tail and he snarled in anger. A few invaders fell back in fear, but the others pressed on. He began to move steadily to the entrance of the cave, taking one deep breath after another, snorting and steaming. He roared his annoyance as their tiny arrows pricked like thorns at his back.

Taking in an enormous gulp of air, he tensed, then lunged past the stragglers and out through the mouth of the cave. Wings spread wide, the lone dragon soared from the hollowed mountain into the cold night air. Driven by

21

rage, he flew until he could go no further; he was shivering and spent by the time he found shelter at last in a thick grove of trees.

At dawn he woke, sleep-dazed and chilled. He stretched, then spread his wings to rise up toward the warm sun. The dragon circled slowly, pondering: to return to his cave in the mountain would bring rest only until the next attack. Where, then, might he go? Surely not to the East. Men came from the East, with their spears and lances, stealing gold and leaving chaos behind. No, he would not go East. To the North, he knew, lay even more cold and desolation, while fiery winds and stinging hot sand waited in the South.

The only direction left was the one toward which he had never ventured: West, beyond the Gray Water. He wheeled and glided, anticipating what might lie ahead. How far would he go? What obstacles would he encounter? If he was not strong enough to make the journey, what would befall him? Then as the bright morning light warmed his broad back and extended wings, he felt a surge of strength: he would follow the sun into the West every day. His decision was made.

The dragon soared high in the thin air, wings set at an angle to save strength. Flying into the rose-red and gold sunset, he wondered: might the sun become closer the farther along he flew? Then, relying on his sense of direction, he continued all night through the black sky to again relish the warmth of the morning sun. That day he passed over the seemingly endless expanse of Gray Water.

With care, he skimmed down close to the rippling

surface for a better look. As he inhaled its bracing, salty odor, a gripping chill reached up to numb his stiffening wings, and with effort he brought himself upward away from the deadly cold.

That night the sun set, not an orange ball bobbing into the sea, but a pale circle that disappeared into towering clouds. Once again he flew by instinct, straight through the storm's darkness, as wind tore at his wings and icy rain beat upon every scale. He was in turn buffeted by gusts and blinded by water, but although his long neck ached, his eyes stung and his lungs burned, he stayed on course. There was simply no turning back.

At last in the early dawn, he felt it from below: warmth. Looking down, he was surprised to see, instead of more water, the green of dense foliage and the haze of morning mists clinging lightly to treetops. Suddenly he tipped one tired wing and circled back for another look at the strange mountain. No trees grew upon it and, flying lower, he saw that its sides were actually stone steps that grew narrower and taller to become a point at the top. He had seen nothing like it before.

Overcome by excitement and exhaustion, he landed clumsily in a clearing. Nearby, leafy branches of a tall tree arched out and down to form a canopy that reminded him of his old cave. He crept beneath it, pulled his wings in around him, and slept a heavy sleep.

His mother died at his birth, and as a baby, Choxco had been slow to speak and walk; as a child, the smallest tasks had given him great difficulty. His people treated him with fond indulgence as he grew into a strong youth who spent his time in the lush forests, his child-mind fascinated by the animals and birds. That day, however, Choxco saw the strangest animal yet.

He thought it was a huge moss-covered boulder under the tree, until its sides flexed with slow breathing and he saw the wings folded along its back. Parting the hanging branches, Choxco drew closer; although very large, the beast was certainly not as terrible and frightening as some of the temple carvings in the city.

"Ah, you are a great bat!" He stroked its leathery gray wings, then noticed the scales that covered the beast's hide. "Or are you a serpent?"

The dragon's tail twitched suddenly, and the young man jumped, startled.

"Aiee! You tricked me! You *are* part serpent." Choxco ran his hand over the dragon's side and looked down at its lizard-like head, eyes firmly closed. "You look sleepy. I will return tomorrow." With that, he trotted out of the clearing. The following day he appeared again, carrying two dead rabbits and a tall pot of water. This time he was rewarded, as the dragon stirred, awoke, then spied the food.

Although Choxco had seen many snakes consume their prey, he had never seen one chewing, and he watched in wonder as the rabbits were devoured. Then he placed the pot of water in front of the dragon; it paused, peered down at its reflection, then thrust its head inside and drank with noisy slurps that echoed inside the pot. Unafraid, Choxco laughed, slapping his hands on his knees.

"You are very funny, Bat-Serpent!" The dragon withdrew its head from the pot, then sat back on its haunches and stretched its neck. "And very tall, too," Choxco added as he looked up. He stepped sideways to see more of the creature, and stumbled over the empty pot. "Oh! I will get more water for you," he said, then picked up the pot and ran out of the clearing. "It is a very big animal and will need a lot to drink," he said to himself. By the time he returned with more water, the animal was again asleep.

"I must go now, Bat-Serpent, but I will come back." Choxco stood up beside the beast, and for the first time, looked closely at its gray-green scales. Soaked by the rain, shredded by the wind, their edges were split and frayed, giving them a downy appearance. When he patted the dragon's side fondly, they tickled his hand and made him laugh.

When the scent of food awakened the dragon, he ate ravenously, then drank all the water in the small well in front of him and scarcely noticed the young man standing nearby. The dragon felt stiff: his neck ached, his eyes were crusted, his wings were sore and raw, even his long tail hurt. He drifted back to sleep with the pleasant realization that at least he was not cold. He awoke briefly at night to the sounds of distant animals, then dozed again until morning. Birds in the treetops made calls he had never heard before, while sunlight twinkled down through bright green leaves. He stretched, yawned, and ventured out of his forest den. After his long flight and longer rest, his legs were wobbly and he did not go far, but sat in the clearing and gazed about. He felt at once comfortable and safe amid the dense greenery, and knew he had made the right choice; here was his new home. His empty stomach growled and rumbled, and only then did he recall the young man who had brought him food and water.

Well toward midday, he grew warmer until thirst overcame hunger. On the forest floor he saw a rough path, with leaves trampled and branches pushed aside; he followed it.

Choxco's father had extra work for him, and it was three long days before he returned to the forest. He made his way to the clearing and peeked behind the curtain of branches, only to sigh with disappointment; the great creature was gone. Only a tiny frog stared up at him.

"You do not fool me," he told it. "You are not the Bat-Serpent." Choxco picked up the empty water jug. "When he comes back he may be thirsty, so I will leave him some water." He turned and made his way down the path to the water.

It trickled from a small spring down the hillside, where it widened into a pool surrounded by flat rocks. Carefully Choxco knelt by the pool, then as he began to fill the pot, an immense cloud blocked the sun. Shading his eyes with his hand, he peered up into the sky, to see not a cloud but the dragon, high overhead.

"You are flying! Here I am, Bat-Serpent!" Gleefully Choxco waved and shouted, his arms held high. Then in one breathless moment, the dragon dove down, grasped the young man's hands firmly in its back claws and again took to the air.

"Aiiiieee!" At once thrilled and startled, Choxco felt a stab of fear, then was exhilarated as he rode along, held aloft by his new winged friend. They skimmed over the trees, then circled around and returned to the pond where he was gently set down, shaking and giddy with excitement. He knelt and scooped up water in cupped hands, while beside him the dragon folded its wings, then likewise bent down and drank its fill.

"Ahh," Choxco said at last. "We were very thirsty, Bat-Serpent." He sat back on the warm rock and looked up at the dragon in admiration. "That was a good game. I would like to go flying with you again someday."

The dragon waved its tail, sending a spray of water over Choxco who shouted with glee. His laughter mingled with the screech of monkeys and the raucous calls of parrots high in the treetops of the lush forest.

As time passed, the dragon flew a bit farther each day across the land, exploring the new terrain. He ate crayfish from the stream and an occasional egg from an unguarded nest. He marveled at the sweet, sugary scent of flowers deep in the jungle, relaxed on sun-baked, flat rocks, and listened fascinated to the rustle and screech of small creatures in the night. Men were here too -- but they tended crops and herded animals, and at night retired quietly to their white, boxy dwellings. He was not attacked nor even bothered, and grew more at ease. No matter how far he ventured, he came always to his clearing, in anticipation of the young man that brought him food and water, that waved and called to him with such joy. The dragon was content.

Natives of the city were followers of Tezcatlipoca, the warrior god who foretold men's futures in battle and determined their destiny. When the city was conquered by another tribe through sheer numbers, they thus found themselves ruled by the high priest of Quetzalcoatl. Also called the Feathered Serpent, he was the god of knowledge and patron of arts, thus the new ruler of the city brought his own skilled stonecarvers, painters, and potters to grace his temple. The priests of Tezcatlipoca despised the outsiders and regarded them as weak and inferior; nevertheless, the artisans lived apart from the city, oblivious to native resentment, and prospered. These were Choxco's people.

His father was a painter who worked each day with brushes and pigment to create murals. They depicted not only Quetzalcoatl in all his grandeur, but panoramas of festivals and rites of passage. To obtain the vivid colors their father preferred, Choxco's sisters ground plants and minerals into powder; many they gathered, but some, more rare, had to be purchased.

That meant a morning at the marketplace, festive with its smells and sights. Choxco went along with his sisters, darting about, lively as a puppy while they searched and bargained. Stopping at the potter's stall, he spied a jug that bore an image of an undulating creature, painted in bright blue and green.

"It is my Bat-Serpent!" Choxco exclaimed, pulling at his sister's hand. "It looks like my friend in the forest!" Left to himself each day, when his simple tasks were finished Choxco went straight to the stream or the clearing. His father and sisters had grown accustomed to his comical stories of the flying serpent.

"Your friend is a lizard?" his younger sister teased.

"It is Quetzalcoatl," the older girl pointed. "See, here are his wings..."

"He flies." Choxco flapped his arms to demonstrate.

"So, it is Quetzalcoatl that waits for you in the forest?"

Choxco nodded vigorously, clapping his hands.

"You are very lucky. We should buy flowers and incense to offer him at his temple."

"The Bat-Serpent is my greatest friend," Choxco declared, nearly bursting with excitement.

All this was of much interest to two priests of Tezcatlipoca who stood nearby. The pair whispered to each other as Choxco and his sisters moved away.

"What does it signify, that Quetzalcoatl waits in the forest?" one asked.

"It must be a plot against Tezcatlipoca," the other answered. Both nodded, the bones and teeth in their headdresses clicking. They hastily returned to their temple and informed the other priests of what they had heard. Wrapped in jaguar-skin cloaks, they sat in council far into the night as torches eerily lit the walls around them. Flames made the painted scenes appear to move: alongside priests clad in bright cloaks, lines of men ascended a stepped pyramid, past butchered, bleeding bodies that lay in grotesque display, to the top where each victim was held down as the high priest sliced open his chest to extract his heart, the ultimate tribute demanded by the fierce god Tezcatlipoca.

By dawn the fate of Choxco was sealed.

The minions of Tezcatlipoca kept a vigil at the temple of Quetzalcoatl and waited with grim patience. Several days passed before one of them noticed a tall, handsome young man accompanied by two young women, leaving offerings of bright flowers and colorful feathers.

"That is the one?" The priest nudged his companion, hidden behind a pillar.

"Yes."

"You are certain."

He nodded, and the two moved forward, confronting Choxco as he left the temple.

"Come with us," said the taller one, as he grabbed Choxco firmly by the arm.

"Where are we going?" Choxco asked him, wide-eyed and smiling.

The priest, who expected a struggle, was taken aback but maintained his grip on the young man. "You must come now." Then as the other priest stepped in front of his sisters, blocking their way, Choxco was led off into the crowd.

Confused and anxious, the two young women stopped everyone who passed by, to ask if their brother had been seen. No one knew; it was as though Choxco had vanished. They returned home frantic, and their father found them in tears when his work day was done. In turn crying and speaking, they told him of the visit to

Quetzalcoatl's temple, then of Choxco's disappearance with the two men.

"Tell me of them," their father said gently.

"One was taller, he held our brother's arm..."

"The other stood in our way, we could not pass..."

"...he said something to Choxco but I could not hear..."

"...then they took him, and we could not see where..." Then neither could speak for weeping.

Their father comforted the girls. "Describe them."

"They wore headdresses of feathers, with bones and teeth that hung down."

"And cloaks of jaguar-skin."

At this, their father's shoulders sagged. "They are priests of Tezcatlipoca. Choxco has been taken to their temple for a sacrifice."

The older sister moaned and held the younger one to her; sacrifice meant only one thing. While followers of Quetzalcoatl performed dances and songs in his honor and left fruit, flowers and works of art, in Tezcatlipoca's honor victims gave their still-beating hearts and left pools of blood.

"We are strangers here and must obey their customs," he continued. "It is a very great honor to their god Tezcatlipoca..." his voice grew faint and he fell silent. Choxco's sisters said nothing, but late that night in the dark they wept and clung to each other in despair, over the foreign god of warriors and the cruel fate of their gentle brother.

On his daily flight across the land, the dragon never

failed to scan the clearing and stream for a glimpse of his friend. After several days passed without a sign of him, early one morning the dragon flew in ever-widening circles looking for the young man who always waved at him so happily. The sky was clear, the sun bright and warm; it was a day of ceremony.

Assembled at the sacrificial pyramid were dignitaries, musicians, and priests of Tezcatlipoca. They wore jaguar-skin cloaks and carried clubs carved with skulls and bones; ornate golden masks covered their faces and reflected the sun's rays in every direction. Singing and chanting, they climbed the steps and circled the green stone altar.

High above, the dragon glided silently until he saw the open space far below where men, a vast number of them, were gathered on one of the pointed mountains. Apprehensive yet curious, he spiraled downward; closer to the crowd, he then saw none other than his friend, being led to a flat green stone. Surrounding the young man were others, wearing great golden masks and holding black stone knives.

Knives, spears, arrows -- they were all tools of men that the dragon knew meant but one thing: pain and injury.

The storm-shredded edges of his scales fluttered and snapped in the rushing air as he swooped down. His shadow loomed above the priests and they scattered like mice, falling down the steps in panic.

Freed, Choxco sprang up and waved excitedly to his friend, oblivious to the pandemonium around him.

"Here I am, Bat-Serpent! Down here!"

The dragon wheeled and descended; slowing, he

reached down and, in the same way they played their game at the stream, took hold of Choxco's upraised hands with his rear claws and flew with him into the forest beyond. The sound of Choxco's excited laughter was drowned out by screams and cries as Tezcatlipoca's followers fled in terror.

High priests of Tezcatlipoca chose sacrificial participants more carefully for a time. From atop their ceremonial pyramids, they posted lookouts for Quetzalcoatl, for although they regarded him as a weak, powerless god that demanded neither blood nor hearts, it was unwise to risk provoking his winged fury.

It was decreed that Choxco become an honored priest of Quetzalcoatl. Although he did his best to be dignified, he still laughed and teased his sisters when they came to leave offerings. One day in every seven he went alone into the forest; it was said by the other priests that there he experienced magnificent visions, for he always returned with colorful tales of the feathered serpent.

Although he thrived in his new land, the dragon grew very old, and the time came when he took to the sky and did not return. Choxco, in his simple trust, always believed the dragon would come back, and that became the most enduring tale of all.

∧∧∧

# THE WALL

It is the thirty-third year in the reign of Shih Huang-ti, our Emperor Most Learned. A comet blazes across the night skies and, after much consultation of books and charts, I perceive something of great importance to come upon the horizon. The comet has come to light its way.
-- Tan T'ian, Court Astrologer

There is still no word from the expedition that our Just and Benevolent Majesty organized, searching for the elixir of immortality. In the meantime the Emperor busies himself with court paperwork, and of course his Imperial dragons. They are beloved by everyone at court, and it falls to me to prepare roasted swallow and other toothsome delicacies for them daily.

One evening a dragon hatchling wandered away from the main hall and disappeared. His Majesty was beside himself, enlisting the aid of the Royal guards to search for the missing one. Even after it was found, curled up asleep behind a lacquer chest, His Majesty was so highly agitated that I thought it beneficial to brew an herbal drink with which to calm him. Our Great and Glorious Emperor believes that, should any dragons escape the land, the good fortune of his reign will vanish with them.

# THE WALL

-- Weng Po, Royal Cook

I was at court today when His Illustrious Majesty became excited as a child concerning a project he wishes to undertake.

'We must protect our Imperial Treasures,' said His Majesty to Prime Minister Li Szu.

'But, Your Majesty,' Li Szu responded (he of the silken tongue), 'all the gold and precious stones are already under heavy guard, please be assured.'

Then in a tone of a schoolmaster addressing a rather dull boy, The Emperor replied, 'No, Li Szu, not jades or gold. The treasures we must protect are, of course, the Royal dragons.' And His Majesty reached down to fondly stroke the small green female dragon that lay at his feet.

'Ah, of course,' Li Szu echoed, pressing his hands together. Our Most Kind Ruler's fondness for dragons is legendary. There will be more to come of this, I am positive.
-- Tan T'ian, Court Astrologer

My kitchen staff has been increased by five, although not to help with tasks of preparing more elegant fare for the court. No -- they are official Royal food-tasters. His Majesty of Enduring Virtue and Goodness has grown apprehensive with the recent attempts on his life, and wants to eat in safety. Far from being offended, I understand, and myself wish good health for His Majesty, may he live long! I served a midday meal to His Majesty yesterday and observed the following procedure: Upon each dish being presented, it was sampled by at least two of the court

tasters. After some minutes with no ill effects noted, portions were given, not to the Emperor but to the dragons seated on his left and right. They had the choicest morsels, while Prime Minister Li Szu (Sour-Plum Face) sat farther away and was served much later. I told Tan T'ian of this and it brought him hearty laughter.
-- Weng Po, Royal Cook

I was casting the Royal monthly horoscope today at court when His Majesty suddenly sent for Li Szu. I arose to leave, but 'No, no, Tan T'ian, there is no need,' said the Emperor, smiling. Then Li Szu entered the chamber, robes flowing, moustache impeccably trimmed, stern face glancing neither left nor right. Bowing low to the emperor, he straightened, barely acknowledged me and then noticed that there was only one other stool before the throne, already occupied by a reddish-gold dragon. Li Szu proceeded to stand throughout the entire audience.

'I have decided that we shall build a wall,' said our Sagacious Ruler.

'Ah, a fortification to repel enemy invaders.' Li Szu nodded enthusiastically.

'No, no, Li Szu,' The Emperor said impatiently. 'A wall to keep our precious treasures from straying.' He stroked the sleeping dragon at his side. 'It need not be very high,' His Majesty continued, 'for after all unlike their ancestors in ages past, they can no longer fly.' At his touch the dragon's small wings flexed and fluttered, thin and fragile as a courtesan's fan.

'But if it were tall, it would also serve as a monument

to His Noble Majesty's greatness,' persisted Li Szu.

'Hm, yes, I suppose.' The Emperor paused, then pointed at the Prime Minister. 'General Meng Tien. He is the man to supervise such an undertaking. You will see to it, Li Szu. That is all.' The Emperor waved one hand, rather like a magician, for by doing so he caused Li Szu to vanish, which all present appreciated.

-- Tan T'ian

Much excitement has taken place at court! Today a grand ceremony was held marking the beginning of construction on the Emperor's wall. A feast followed, at which I had the great good fortune to be present, as His Majesty The Virtuous gave a speech on the importance of the Court Dragons, stressing the responsibility we all share to maintain and protect them. Then Li Szu spoke, praising His Majesty at length of course, and eloquently predicting that the wall would prove to be of significant military value. Li Szu uses events and words as a potter does clay pieces, twisting and turning them to suit his own ends.

-- Weng Po

It is the thirty-fifth year in the reign of our Illustrious Emperor Powerful and Strong. In the nine years I have served as Court Astrologer, no events have disquieted me as those I see now. There is growing persecution of those who teach the Old Ways, instigated by none other than Li Szu. Learning is considered suspect, and as a result many scholars have left the court for distant provinces. Those remaining wait to hear the words of the Emperor, only to nod their heads in safe, unthinking agreement.

With each passing moon, our Emperor, he whom the gods shower with their blessings, becomes more clouded in his thinking. Currently he has decided that his whereabouts must be kept secret outside the palace. Moreover, walkways between his dwellings are to be covered, thus deceiving the evil spirits that stalk him.
All this saddens me for I respect His Majesty greatly. I must visit Weng Po, who never fails to cheer my heart as well as my stomach.
-- Tan T'ian


Oh my, I am most shaken, and have had some wine before even attempting to write. I was in the ornamental bamboo grove, pursued by the large red male dragon. It is a game we play: he chases me and nips at the hem of my trousers, whereupon I stop and he releases me. We were resting for a moment when I head voices from a nearby doorway.

'People speak of rebellion, of escaping to the north,' said a voice unfamiliar to me. 'It will mean less tax revenue and fewer laborers...'

'I will make sure that The Wall is finished, and soon!' That voice I recognized immediately: it was Li Szu. 'It will keep rebels in, as well as foreigners out,' he spat.

'But the Emperor believes The Wall is being erected only to contain the dragons, doe he not?'

'Leave the Emperor to me. You are to complete The Wall with utmost speed.'

Footsteps faded away, then silence. I uttered prayers

to the Nine Regions of Heaven that the red dragon would not snort and betray us both, and thanks be, he kept quiet. Oh, my, this is all very confusing. I believe I shall have some more wine.

-- Weng Po

Chao Yun, the nobleman in whose court I was employed before entering into the Emperor's service, visited today. It grew warm, and he suggested we enjoy the shade of some chestnut trees at the east end of the gardens. I soon leaned this was a ruse to put us far from the palace; my visitor had disquieting news to relate.

'More than one source reports overwork and cruelty in the treatment of those laboring on The Wall.' At my shocked silence, Chao Yun continued. 'The placement of The Wall is also most irregular, on jagged rocks that protrude from the earth. This makes shorter the distance it traverses, but is contrary to the Natural Way of Wind and Water. Tan T'ian, were you aware of these transgressions?'

So surprised was I, I could only shake my head dumbly. 'This is most inauspicious,' Chao Yun said, then took my arm and suggested we return to the palace before we were missed and sent for by one of Li Szu's minions. Weng Po had prepared a most elaborate meal in honor of our noble visitor, but I recall nothing of what I ate. I am most disquieted.

--Tan T'ian

Now this is a puzzle! I have heard that, at great expense and with tremendous manpower, work has begun on the Emperor's tomb. I posed the question to Tan T'ian, if our Just and Benevolent Majesty expects to live forever, why does he need a tomb? The Astrologer laughed then.

The Emperor's most recent expedition in search of the elixir of immortality has returned empty-handed; I personally know of no food or drink that will guarantee eternal life.

For myself, I do not wish to live forever. The snows of universal winter will one day cover my ancient bones for the last time. That is how it should be.

Now I hear a grunting and squeaking from the darkened kitchen. I must go and feed the small dragons their last bit of food for the night.

-- Weng Po


I am my own undoing and will surely be sent to prison to suffer the Five Tortures!

The Emperor, His Majesty Most Merciful, instructed me to consult the charts regarding his upcoming grand tour of inspection. I did so and produced a forecast most auspicious for his travels. Only after His Majesty's entourage had departed, did I discover that I had based my reading on the Year of the Monkey, and we are still in the Year of the Ram! Numerous will be the punishments inflicted upon me, I have no doubt.

Worse yet, I wrote out the entire forecast upon a scroll for His Majesty to take on the journey. Along with poems and essays, it is rolled and tied with my special knot and bears one of my court insignias. I may as well have written, 'Tan T'ian is a fool no longer capable of his post.' His

Majesty has sent men's heads home in boxes for lesser transgressions. With all good fortune I will merely be sent to labor on The Wall.

    -- Tan T'ian

Terrible, terrible day. A dispatch was received from the temple astrologer in a northern province. He expressed surprise at seeing His Majesty, respectfully noting that it was not the most fortuitous time for traveling. Whereupon, Tan T'ian's scroll was produced and his mistake disclosed.

His Majesty has conveyed his dissatisfaction in terms most unpleasant. Tan T'ian will not be consoled, he talks only of imprisonment and torture. My head aches so that I cannot write more.

    -- Weng Po

Weng Po constantly reassures me, thought I panic anew with each Royal communication. Rumors have reached us that the Emperor's actions grow ever more unreasonable: upon encountering soldiers on the road, he asked them the name of their commander, and when they failed to say it was himself, the Emperor had their right hands cut off. My respect for His Majesty is turning more to fear with each day.

    --Tan T'ian

Now I will write, although doing so make my hand shake badly. I have unburdened myself to Tan T'ian, who is agitated as am I. The events were these:

Late last night, I heard carts arrive in the back

courtyard. Although thinking it an unusual hour for supplies to be delivered, I arose and ventured out into the torchlit yard. People were most rapid in deportment, strangely quiet, talking in whispers with an air of urgency. Nearby was a covered cart reeking of bad fish; I was ready to seek out the driver and refuse the shipment, when I saw it.

The Imperial Litter, emblazoned with the Celestial Five-Clawed Dragon of Wisdom. Being so close, I desired only to see inside, to glimpse the richness of brocade, the elegance of beaded draperies tied back with decorative tassels, of which I had heard stories. Such opportunities do not occur often! So, after furtive looks to each side, I pulled back the curtain and peeked in.

There sat our Sovereign Illustrious Emperor. I scarcely breathed, not wishing to awaken him, then my hair wriggled as with winter lice, as I realized that His Majesty was not asleep. Alas, he had not discovered the Secret of Immortality on his journey. His smell rivaled that of the cartful of fish, for Our Esteemed Emperor was very, very dead.

Releasing the curtain, I jumped back in horror and hid behind an orange tree. Four guards returned at that instant and bore the Imperial Litter into the Royal chambers. Unseen in the confusion, I made my way back to my chamber, where sleep eluded me.

Just after dawn, Li Szu formally announced that 'Our Right and Moral Majesty returned to his palace late last night where, to the Sorrow of the Heavens, he died quite suddenly.'

Ha! So clever! In accordance with court procedure, Most High Scheming Weasel Li Szu thus assumes the mantle of Royal powers. Ah, me. At least Tan T'ian need not fear reprisals; Li Szu may be devious but his mind is still intact.

--Weng Po

In the ninth month of the thirty-eighth year of his reign, His Majesty Shih-Huang-ti was buried in his tomb, with the pomp and ceremony befitting our Revered Emperor. The great tiger slumbers peacefully now for eternity.

I do not care for the role-playing politics of Li Szu. Indeed, ambition may prove more dangerous than the workings of an addled mind. I have been invited to return to the court of Chao Yun, and have accepted his most generous offer.

--Tan T'ian

Uncounted are the banquets I have prepared here at the Royal Palace. None were undertaken with the mingled joy and sadness as the farewell repast for Tan T'ian, since for me it signaled the loss of a friend and confidant. The feast was attended by the few remaining elder scholars and dignitaries who had served along with the Court Astrologer. Li Szu sent apologies as he had another engagement; no one missed him and the dragons were given his chair.

The task of seeing to the Royal Dragons is now mine alone. It is in the evenings when I am with them that I have fondest recollections of His Majesty. He would join me and dole out bits of food to all, bestowing special affection upon each one. To him they were truly precious beyond measure. They miss him, as, I confess, now do I.

--Royal Cook, Weng Po

Accompanied by guards and courtiers, I departed yesterday for the court of Chao Yun. I left with considerable sadness, for Weng Po is as a brother to me and no day will pass without thoughts of him.

Today I at last saw The Wall. Massive in height, it rises and falls like the spine of an immense beast. It is, I believe, His Majesty's greatest accomplishment. While outside roam the barbarian invaders, within the Middle Kingdom, cared for by faithful Weng Po the cook, safely dwell our Imperial Treasures, the Royal Dragons.

--Court Astrologer, Tan T'ian

∧∧∧

# POMEGRANATE

Branches of the great pomegranate tree reached upward, like gnarled fingers of an aged hand. In a wide place near the center, green leaves parted to reveal bright scales iridescent in the midday sun. The dragon spread and folded his wings contentedly, then, arching his long neck, gazed at the view from his tree.

On the slope in the garden below, carefully tended artichokes flourished in between fig and olive trees, and grape vines grew abundantly inside a low stone fence. In the distance, at the bottom of the hill, was the well. Shaded by date palms, the caravans of merchants, tribesmen and travelers sought rest and refreshment, season upon season, as it had ever been, at the oasis of Ayah-Djin.

The dragon turned his attention to voices, laughing and calling out, coming closer and closer. Two young people raced up the narrow road, catching each other then breaking free again in mock pursuit. As they neared the tree they argued playfully.

"Hadam, stop, I have no more breath," begged the young woman. "You run swift as a goat."

"You are the goat, Anif, and a silly one too," the young man laughed, turning to her. "You believed the silk merchant's tale of the jackal." He reached the shade beneath the pomegranate tree and sank down, resting against its trunk.

"I did not believe him," she replied indignantly as she straightened her tunic and pushed a lock of hair from her eyes. "I was doing as the Wise One taught us, to listen to all and respect their words."

The dragon craned his neck, peering down at them through half-closed amber eyes.

"It is time for midday rest, yet I cannot sleep, with two young donkeys squabbling beneath my tree," he said sternly.

The two looked upward into the green leaves with fondness. Anif placed her hand on the weathered bark of the tree as she spoke.

"Wise One, did you not teach us to listen and learn from all who pass through Ayah-Djin, and thus gain knowledge?"

"Yesss," came the sibilant reply.

"But, Wise One, what is learned from listening to fool's tales?" Hadam retorted impatiently.

"There may be a great deal to learn," answered the dragon. "Tell me this fool's tale."

"Once..."

"There was..." Both began to speak at once.

"One may speak, the other must wait," the dragon said sternly. Anif looked down at her sandals, while Hadam cleared his throat and started again.

"At the well today, the silk merchant told a story about the jackal who became so angered at being outwitted by the hound, that he ate himself up, starting with his own tail, until there was nothing left."

After a moment, the dragon asked, "Is there more to the story?"

Hadam shook his head. "No. But Anif is a fool, because she believed it!"

There was a rustling of leaves and small branches as the dragon rearranged his long tail. "Anif, do you truly believe such a thing could come to pass?"

"Indeed not," she scoffed, flinging a small handful of leaves on Hadam. "But hearing the merchant tell of it was magical. He changed his voice, speaking as each animal, and his words came quick then slow, until the tale seemed almost real. I did not believe it, it is a child's story." So saying, she picked up a tiny pebble and tossed it at Hadam's foot. Then both fell silent and waited, faces turned upward.

"Often even a child's story contains a small pearl of wisdom," the dragon said at length. "Have you never seen one who is so filled with anger within his heart that it consumes him?"

As Hadam and Anif pondered his question, the dragon settled into his nest in the tree. Tired from their chase and made drowsy by the midday sun, the young pair leaned against each other as sleep overcame them.

Hadam awoke with Anif's cheek upon his shoulder as she slept. He put out his hand, palm flat against the tree.

"Wise One..." There was no answer but Hadam continued. "I do not think Anif a fool...I only made jest with her today." He curved his arm protectively around the young woman's shoulder. At a distant tinkling of bells, he shaded his eyes with his other hand and looked down the hill.

"Awake, Anif." He gave her shoulder a nudge, then shook her gently. "Shepherds approach the oasis. We shall help them to water their flocks and refresh themselves, then perhaps they will barter with the silk merchants..."

"...and tonight there will be a feast!" Anif finished, sitting up. "I am sure, Wise One, no one will miss a few tender pieces of lamb from the cooking fires." She tipped her head back and winked.

"Ahh," the dragon responded with a contented yawn. "Wisdom occasionally has its rewards."

The time of harvest came, as once more Hadam and Anif labored to put by their store of almonds, olives, dried fruit and grain from the garden. By tending flocks for the herders and bartering with the caravans, they lived as the Wise One had taught them over the years, in comfort and peace with all who came to the oasis of Ayah-Djin.

Kept busy at their tasks, it had been several days since the two had visited the pomegranate tree. Leaves were turning to gold as the fruit began to change from green to red, heavy with juice in bright crunchy seeds. Anif fairly twitched with anticipation, waiting for her first taste.

Hadam watched her reach up to the ripening globes. "Every year it is the same," he laughed. "You cannot make them turn red by touching them. You have to wait."

"I remember when I was a child and picked one before it was ripe," Anif admitted, making a sour face.
"The Wise One said indeed there are many ways to learn patience, and many more to learn the truth."

"There are pilgrims at the oasis who say they know the one truth," said Hadam. "They are staying on, waiting for more of their number to come before they continue."

"Have they flocks?" Anif asked.

"They have nothing," said Hadam. "They say their god will provide for their needs."

"Which god is that? All who pass through Ayah-Djin worship their own gods."

"They say it is the one god. You can ask them, their tents are by the oasis. You will know them by the long rough robes they wear."

The following afternoon Hadam walked slowly up the hill. Upon reaching the great tree, he placed his hand on the worn bark.

"Wise One..." he said hesitantly, looking up.

"Yesss?"

"What is 'naked' ?" The words came awkwardly.

"Hmmm," the dragon rumbled. "Where did you learn this puzzling word, young one?"

"The pilgrims at the oasis. When I spoke with them, they pointed their fingers at me and said I was nearly naked and should clothe myself." He pulled at his short silk tunic and straightened his broad shoulders. "Am I not clothed?"

"You dress as do the tribesmen and herders in this land." Stretching his neck, the dragon turned his great head this way and that, as he considered Hadam's apparel. "I am not usually concerned about such matters," he added with a wave of his tail.

"Wise One?" Hadam asked again.

"Yesss?"

"What is 'sin' ?"

"SSSssin?" the dragon echoed, hissing a bit.

"When I said that Anif and I lived together, the pilgrims asked if we had been joined, and I told them we had lived together since we were children. They said we were living in sin. I told them we live here, in the garden, not in sin." Hadam sat down beneath the tree, arms resting upon his knees.

"Never before have I heard these things," the dragon said after a moment, waving his tail slowly back and forth. "What of Anif, does she speak with these pilgrims?"

Hadam shook his head. "The pilgrim women keep to themselves much of the time."

"Why? Are they 'naked' ?"

After Hadam's laughter had ceased, he spoke no more of pilgrims. The dragon settled comfortably into his nest, and together they watched the sunset, red-orange above the distant palm trees meeting the purple-black of the horizon.

The day that followed was warm for harvest time, and Anif brought her midday meal to eat in the shade of the tree.

"Alone today?" asked the Wise One.

"Hadam is again in the company of the pilgrims," she answered, breaking off a piece of bread. "Although they speak of things he does not seem to understand, he is curious about them."

"Are you not curious as well?"

"I was curious about a bee, as a child. Then it stung me." Anif took a drink from her water jug.

"Learning can be a painful thing," said the dragon. A soft chuckle mixed with the swish of leaves.

Anif finished her bread and cheese in silence, looking down at the oasis. It was some time before the dragon noticed she had gone.

Afternoon shadows shifted and stretched beneath the pomegranate tree. From above, the dragon watched Hadam trudge along the path, at last halting at the tree. Hadam leaned against the trunk without speaking.

"You are troubled?" the dragon asked.

"I told the pilgrims that Anif and I learn from you," Hadam began, hesitant. "They do not believe that you guide us. They say it cannot be, that we cannot speak with you, because you are not as we are."

"None of us is as any other," came the calm reply. "Does that mean none can learn?" Heavy globes of fruit bobbed on branches as the dragon shifted his weight.

The sound of hushed voices and footsteps approaching made Hadam turn. A group of pilgrims had come straggling up the narrow road to the hilltop; now they clustered nearby, whispering as they watched him. One man, more bold than the rest, spoke.

"Is this where you live?"

"The garden gives us food," Hadam replied, as he pointed at the land and the trees below. "We barter with the herdsmen and merchants for our other needs."

" 'We' ? Who lives with you?"

"Anif, my companion."

"Have you been joined, in the temple?"

"I do not know of this 'joining,' " Hadam answered, shaking his head. "We have no temple, only a tent near the oasis."

One of the women made a disapproving sound, and frowned as she pulled at her long robe. Another stepped closer to the pomegranate tree.

"From this tree you learn wisdom?" she asked, looking up into the branches.

"No, not from the tree..." Hadam began. The pilgrims moved closer, some watching him and the rest staring up at the tree. The frowning woman grabbed hold of a pomegranate hanging near her.

"Is this good to eat?" she demanded, pulling at the fruit.

"It is not yet ripe. Until it is red like a ruby, you cannot pick it," Hadam explained.

"It is forbidden?" persisted the woman, still tugging at the pomegranate.

"No, it is..." Hadam started to reply. At that moment the dragon thrust his head out of the branches.

"Do not pick the fruit from the tree until it is ripe!" he hissed impatiently. As he spoke, his long green tail drooped down alongside the tree and wrapped around the trunk for balance.

"Eeeee!" the woman screeched, as she let go of the pomegranate and jumped back. "A serpent!"

The group retreated a short distance, with shouts of alarm.

"It is a serpent!"

"A serpent is in the tree!" The man who had spoken

to Hadam grabbed a rock and threw it, aiming at the leafy center of the tree. The others picked up small rocks and sharp stones and began to hurl them at the tree. Some struck the dragon and still others hit Hadam, who shielded himself with his hands.

"No! You are wrong!" he shouted. "Stop, you do not understand!" Still more stones flew, all aimed at the upper tree branches. With a sudden grunt and a snort, the dragon climbed swiftly to the top, spread his wings, and took flight.

"It is a winged serpent! Run!"

"It will kill us!"

"It will eat us!"

Now truly terrified, the pilgrims scattered in all directions, running and screaming.

"You must come with us!" The man who had thrown the first rock grasped Hadam's wrist tightly.

"But this is my home," protested Hadam, confused.

"You must leave this place or you will burn in eternal fire!" shrieked the frowning woman.

"But..." Hadam hesitated, then he was pushed and shoved along with the crowd as they stampeded down the hill to their camp.

Gradually all the sounds of panic faded and dust settled along the road. All was quiet once more as Anif stepped cautiously from behind a massive fig tree, looking first up the road, then down. Assured she was alone, she returned to the pomegranate tree and cleared away all the stones. Then she smoothed the trampled ground and sat down to wait.

It was twilight before she heard the familiar sound,

like a camel blanket flapping in the wind. Strong, supple wings bore the dragon back to his tree, then strong claws dug into bark on heavy branches at the edge of his nest.

"Are they gone?" he asked, blowing out gusts of steam.

"Yes, Wise One," Anif replied anxiously. "Are you hurt?"

"Never before have I encountered pilgrims such as these! They are quite rude and disrespectful," the dragon declared, ignoring her question.

"Perhaps their one god does not bring them happiness."

"Then they should try another," he grumbled, settling himself. "Serpent, indeed," he huffed, and winced as a tree branch scraped his bruised foreleg.

"Hadam...went with them," Anif added hesitantly.

"Hmmmmmf." The dragon gave a long, steamy sigh.

"I will go and find him tonight to be sure that...that he is safe." She leaned against the tree trunk. "We were happy here, before they came. Now..." she looked up into the branches and beyond, at the early stars high in the eastern sky, then went on.

"When we were young, you bid us build the stone fence, to keep the donkeys from eating the artichokes and grape vines..."

"Mmm..."

Anif continued wistfully. "I wish we could build a wall around us..."

"You cannot keep people out as easily as donkeys, young one," the dragon said gently.

Anif did not reply, but looked down at the glowing fires of tribesmen. As dusk closed around the hill, she made her way back to the oasis.

It was the middle of the night; the moon was a mere melon-slice, low in the sky. The crunch of hesitant footsteps nearby alerted the dragon, high in his nest, but he was startled to hear Hadam call to him in a husky whisper.

"Wise One? Are you there?"

"Of courssssssssse," the dragon replied.

"I am so glad," Hadam sighed with relief. "Please, allow me to apologize for today, I did not know they would..."

"You are not responsible for their actions, nor their words. Let them think what they will."

Hadam twisted the edge of his cloak nervously. "I have persuaded them to leave..."

"Good riddance," the dragon snapped.

"Please, Wise One, I have to explain, they all met together and their leader told them to return to the garden, to come here and destroy everything..."

As the dragon gave a snort of fury, Hadam continued, whispering urgently.

"...they vowed to kill you. That is when I told them I would go with them, listen to them, and learn about their one god, but only if they agreed to depart the next day, and leave the garden untouched."

There was no sound from the pomegranate tree, not even the shaking of a single leaf.

"I will miss this place, and you most of all. I will not remain with them forever, Wise One. Now I must go, before

Anif awakes and finds me gone," Hadam finished hurriedly, then vanished in the dark.

At sunup the next day, attired in a camel driver's headdress and long cloak, Anif stood beneath the tree.

"Wise One? I know it is early..."

"I am already awake," the dragon said quietly.

"The pilgrims are leaving." She paused, then all her words poured out at once. "They say Ayah-Djin is an evil place where people go naked and observe sinful practices."

"It seems that evil appears in all they behold," the dragon added, his tone subdued.

"Hadam is leaving with them." Anif looked upward, blinking back tears. "Their words have changed him somehow. I think that is why he is going with them." She put her face in her hands and began to cry. The dragon's tail draped down gently around her shoulders as she went on sadly, sniffing. "I too am going. I do not wish to leave, in my heart. This is my home, here, in the garden, with you. But Hadam has always been by my side, since we came here as children, lost from the slave caravan. I cannot think of life without him."

"Even when he teases you and says you are a fool?" the dragon asked gently.

Anif laughed then, and wiped her eyes with a corner of her cloak. "Yes, even then. He is as a part of me."

The dragon sighed. "Tell me, then, do you also believe in their god?" he asked.

"No!" Anif stared straight up at the dragon, her eyes blazing. "Those people are as sheep, following blindly after whoever leads them. I will not be led." She drew her cloak in and crossed her arms. "As long as I am at Hadam's side, I will never let him forget how beautiful our life was here, with you in the garden."

With a parting caress of his tail, the dragon climbed higher into the tree. Anif watched as branches shook, then from the topmost branch, she saw strong claws pluck a single ruby-red pomegranate, ripened by the harvest sunshine. It fell straight to her in a shower of yellow leaves.

"A gift, from me."

"Oh, thank you, " she laughed, catching it in her cloak. Anif tucked the fruit safely into her tunic.

"I..." she could not speak for a moment. "We will never forget you." With one last upward glance, she held her hand against the worn tree trunk in farewell, then turned and started down the road. From high in his nest, the dragon watched Anif depart, her steps firm and her head high.

Ages passed, and over time the caravans ceased coming to Ayah-Djin; many forgot it even existed. The Wise One looked for Hadam and Anif at every harvest season when the pomegranates were red and ripe, but neither ever returned to the garden.

∧∧∧

# <u>PLAGUE</u>

Wark the cobbler was stifling under his bedcovers. Plague was upon the country once again and the night air was thick with it; he would surely be stricken were he to open the shutters. As he tossed and turned, a scurrying and squealing outside his windows made him lay still, cupping one knobby hand to his ear.

Witches! Witches, flying to a sabbat! What else could be about in the dark of night when God-fearing people were in their beds? Wark clutched his rough covers under his bearded chin. He had never seen a witch, except of course the one they tried last year in town, an unremarkable specimen at that, plain of face, not even a wart upon her...But he had heard tales of them, aye, riding their broomsticks across the skies with black cats perched on their humped backs. Wark recalled the one last year had no hump at all...ah, but the witches that flew through the skies, oft it was told, rode naked! Naked they were, their pendulous sagging breasts swaying in the moonlight as they traveled to their trafficks with The Devil himself...

Suddenly Wark sat bolt upright, dry reeds in his mattress crunching under his weight. Driven by the possible specter of breasts, sagging or otherwise, he arose and made his way to the window at front of his shop. Stiff

fingers fumbled with the latch on the wicker shutters as curiosity prodded him. 'Twas, after all, his duty to God to verify such unearthly goings-on. With a scratchy creak, the shutter opened a crack affording Wark a pinched view of the street outside.

No hags rent the skies. An oval moon gave enough illumination to outline thatched roofs above. Then Wark glanced down at the gutters below his window and gasped.

Cats! Hundreds of them! Wark counted at least a dozen as they busily plied the streets, their footpads making scant sound as they tracked and dispatched their prey. Squeaks from victims accompanied random yowls, as the cats disputed territories. Wark felt his skin crawl under his coarse nightshirt as one ran growling beneath his window, a fat black rat held firmly in its mouth. Activity gradually dwindled as the moon traveled its course. Wark groaned at length, stiff from standing on one place for so long, then jerked himself upright; as the moon disappeared, so would the cats! Witches familiars they were, vanishing before day break as they always did, it was common knowledge. He rubbed rheumy eyes, straining for a better look. The cats were gone.

In a panic, Wark pulled the shutter closed and fastened it tight, clapping both hands over his mouth. He had breathed the poisonous night air whilst he spied on the cats!

"Pray God the plague not seize me," he mumbled, shaking as he climbed back into his rude bed. Something, he vowed, must be done about the cats. Wark sighed with disappointment over not having seen any witches' breasts,

then fell asleep.

At daybreak Wark arose, stretching and scratching. Already carts and oxen rumbled by and dogs barked. At the memory of the street's occupants the previous night, Wark jerked his shoes on, dressed hastily and ventured out. As he made his way toward the tavern at the end of town, squinting in the sun, he narrowly avoided a farmer's cart as it passed by.

"Have a care!" he shouted, irritable from lack of sleep.

"Look aright, poke-nose," the driver called back.

"Young sprout," Wark grumbled. As he approached the inn, his nose indeed found a target: fat young rabbits roasting on a spit in the fireplace. The aroma drew him in straight away.

Seated at a table was just the person upon whom Wark might bestow his important information. He pulled off his shapeless woolen cap as he confronted the provost.

"Your honor, I would take but a moment to speak with you if 'twould please..."

Nearby the blacksmith and the tailor shared an early pitcher of ale. They nudged each other and fell quiet to eavesdrop on Wark's news.

"Yes, good man?" the provost replied.

Wark pulled up a stool and began in earnest. "This night past, hearing a noise most strange, I looked out my window..."

"Aye Wark, mind ye tell us all, now..."

"Naught gets past our cobbler!" the smith and the tailor rejoined. Indeed, the cobbler's constant surveillance of the street was well-known, and the townsfolk referred

to anything that protruded from a window as 'the cobbler's nose.'

"Pray continue," the provost urged.

"Cats, my lord! The street filled with them, intent on their ungodly journeys. Witches' familiars they are, one and all, consorting with Satan himself, 'tis a fact."

"Ah." Nodding and assent from all present inspired Wark further. "We need be rid of these creatures, just as with God's help we defeated the scourge of witchcraft in year past."

At mention of the witch, coughs and muffled laughter ensued. It seemed that Neaton Clegg accused one Sarah Brines of bewitching his cow so its leg went crooked. The provost and justice of the peace heard his case, and with due procedure installed the protesting woman in the ducking stool over the town pond to test her innocence. Thrice she was ducked into the pond and came up sputtering, before Pirtle Jenks came on the scene and avowed the cow was born with a bent leg. He knew, as it was himself that sold it to Neaton Clegg. The justice found against Clegg, whereupon all went home including the purported witch, still sopping wet and muttering. Many regarded the entire episode as generally foolish and hardly cited it as a moral victory. Nevertheless, encouraged at having audience with the provost, Wark continued his speech.

"Next night but one will bring a full moon, an' bodes well for confronting these imps of Beelzebub."

"Aye, aye!" the assembled company warmed to the task.

"What about plague, Wark?" the tailor asked. "Dare we venture out in the night with plague about?" The tavern grew silent as this problem was pondered.

"The plague is God's punishment for our sins," droned the morose churchman seated in a far corner.

"Well then, stands to reason, 'twould make for a mighty indulgence were we to catch a witch!" reasoned the tailor, setting his tankard down firmly on the table. "God should forgive us something for that, by all faith."

It seemed a fair bargain to all present, and plans were agreed upon. Wark volunteered to keep watch, which surprised no one.

"Mind ye, keep a sharp eye, now."

"Aye, do your duty, Wark."

The tavern's customers returned to their shops and trades amid chuckling and banter. Wark peeked sideways at the barmaid as she bent to sweep breadcrumbs off the wide table.

Breasts had she, now, and not sagging neither...Wark's hand stole to his chin in rapt concentration, then began to reach out as she bent further over the table, her round bottom swaying 'neath her skirts.

"Have a care now, Wark," she sang out cheerfully, retrieving the long bread knife from her tray. "Cobblers want all their fingers, I daresay."

Wark recoiled and clutched his tankard with both hands, draining the last drop, then dutifully left for his shop, sighing over a lost opportunity.

Excitement mounted as dusk settled on the eve of full moon. Apprehension over breathing plague-infested air was overcome by the urgency of the matter. Wark stoked his fire, making certain he would be ready, sweat streaming down his face in the confined quarters. At intervals he listened for noises outside, and at last he detected scampering along with muffled squeaks. Once again Wark carefully opened his shutter and again witnessed the cats hunting in the deserted street. Wark fairly danced to the fire, lit his torch, seized a nearby tall stick, and burst from his front door.

"Alarm, alarm! Cats, cats!" His neighbors' doors flew open and in minutes the street was in confusion, men running first one direction, then another, cats in full rout. Torchlight, reflected off whitewashed shopfronts, gave the scene an eerie glow. Inadvertently scores of rats were trampled in the fray, and the baker's hair was singed by his torch. Wark, determined to run down his quarry, pursued a large white cat down an alley where it halted. Its back to a fence, it drew itself up tall before him, bright green eyes each with a dark slit in center, staring at him boldly. Then it hissed at him, its mouth drawn wide. Wark raised his stick just as his torch went out. He gave a terrified yelp and flailed about with his stick, but by the time his eyes could see in the moonlight, the cat had vanished.

Unnerved, Wark peered from the alley. Yonder near the well a noisome victory bonfire was being kindled. The campaign had netted countless dead rats and only one cat, an old grizzled one-eared thing, but was considered a success by all. The smell of burning hair rose into the night and fears of plague-ridden air were forgotten at least for the time being.

"Hi, hi, hi! Here's to Wark, our lookout!" Giddy with triumph, the men cheered as Wark entered the firelight. He reveled in the momentary gratitude, calculating that it should bring not a few rounds of ale at the tavern in days to come and perhaps another meeting with the barmaid. As the fire died out, the participants retired for the night, confident that they had purged their town of the Devil's unholy grip once more and in doing so staved off the plague at least until next moon. Not one pointed out that nary a witch had been seen.

A fortnight had passed since the cat raid. The Saturday evening trade in the tavern was brisk, with a handful of revelers dancing to the tailor's tin whistle. Wark managed a few sprightly steps with the barmaid, to the merriment of the crowd; then, out of breath, he sank onto a bench at the far end of a long table. Next to him sat the miller, who stared fixedly at his tankard and looked up only briefly at Wark.

"Ah, friend cobbler," the miller began, with a deep hiccup. "An' it puzzles, me, I do tell you, devils though they were and no mistake now, with the cats gone, I feared the rats would do me in, them being in my grain all night long, as likely." He regarded Wark with befuddlement and rambled on. "Since, I've spied but one or two, an' scarce a bag has been nibbled at of my barley and oats..." He shook his head, again looking down into his ale.

The tailor joined them, clapping the miller on the back heartily. "'Tis God's way of giving you a reward," he put in, then called out, "Bring us another!"

The barmaid promptly replenished the empty pitcher and the miller's consternation was ignored as all fell to sampling the ale.

Thus it was that Wark trod a slow and wavering path homeward very late of an evening. As he stumbled, he put out a hand to catch himself on a rough fencepost, and squinted across the darkened square at the well. A rat disappeared around the smooth stone sides and squeaked once as something moved along the topmost edge.

"Ay, poxy cat!" Wark tossed a pebble at the lip of the well, and heard a *splunk*. As he took aim with another, a head and neck rose up out of the masonry, most un-catlike, undulating to its full length, stretching long and low to the ground to capture yet another rodent. It was the serpent of the Devil, Wark was sure of it, there to tempt him just as it had in the Bible! First the cats, now this unholy torment set upon his soul!

"Yi-i-i-i!" Nearly tripping in clumsy panic, the cobbler made straight for the safety of his own door without looking back. The next day being Sunday, while he did not attend church, he kept inside ministering to his aching head and swearing off ale.

By the next week, the plague was nearer yet. Wark itched and scratched as fleas in his bedding gave him no respite; unable to sleep, he lay listening for noises outside. No cats this time to be sure, all having fled to more tranquil surroundings, but a soft swishing sound...again...and again. Curious, Wark undid the shutters and looked out into the darkness.

"Paugh," he snorted in disgust. Black rats scampered

past the door, next to the white walls, and across the streets. Wark scratched at his chafed skin as he began to secure the shutters tight; it was then he heard the splashing, and let the shutter swing open.

It made its way out of the well, and down the center of the narrow street. First came one foot, then another, then another...with a sound much like a sack of grain being dragged along the cobblestones, it moved slowly but determined. Wark's eyes burned, held wide to be certain of what he was seeing, for he disbelieved it himself. The full moon lay silver light upon the great wings folded across its wide back, as the dragon moved along. It paused to gobble up every rat that crossed its path, neat and silent. As it neared his shop, Wark made to hide behind the shutter, but too late, for it fixed him with an evil gaze, its eyes green with a black slit in center. Its strong neck swayed and arched, up, up, until it towered above the hapless cobbler. Then, its serpent mouth agape, the dragon roared out a deafening belch that sent Wark scurrying.

With a screech, he flew into his bed, covers pulled over him, the fleas in his blankets feasting mightily. There he stayed, quaking anew with every passing hour, not from cold but fear. Throughout the long night, only twice did he peek out at the window, half-expecting the dragon to crash through the wicker shutters and gobble him up right where he lay.

Never had Wark been as grateful for sunrise, as though the light were a talisman against dragons. Bones aching and wits dulled from lack of sleep, the cobbler headed straight for his place of solace and safety: the tavern.

Finding it still closed  and shuttered, Wark rapped upon the door and called plaintively until Jack the tavern keeper lifted the latch.

One look at the cobbler convinced him that all was not well: Wark was bleary-eyed and shaking, dressed in only nightshirt and trousers, and clearly distressed.

"Come, come, friend. Sit here, by the fire." He guided Wark to a stool by the hearth. "Let me get you a tankard of warm cider."

Calmed somewhat,Wark at last turned to his host.

"Last night..." he began, then cleared his throat.  "I saw it plain... eating up the rats, it was... stretching its long neck down, with its wings folded..." his voice trailed off and he stared into the fire.

"Hold now, Wark: long neck? Wings? What could..."

Wark sighed. "Twas a dragon."

A moment of silence was followed by laughter.

"An' now, get on, Wark," Jack teased, poking him in the shoulder. "Says he's seen a dragon," he called to the barmaid, as he stoked the fire.

"So I heard," she answered cheerfully. "No more ale for you of a night, next you'll be knocking before the cock crows, with your dreams o'harpies and imps."

"Twas no dream," Wark insisted earnestly.

The barmaid threw on her cloak and took a basket on her arm. "Bread will be ready at the baker's," she called to Jack as she unlocked the door.

"Come straight back - mind you watch for the dragon!" he answered, still laughing. Then he noticed Wark's demeanor: the blustering cobbler, good-natured butt of many a joke, sat hunched at the fireside, brow wrinkled with worry, hands gripping his cider mug and staring fixedly into the flames. Were the dragon real or imagined, Wark had got no sleep that night, it was plain.

"Here, Wark." Jack helped the cobbler up and guided him to a bench against the wall. "Rest a bit now."
Wark sank down onto the smooth wood, and had but put his feet up when he began to snore undisturbed, until the midday crowd assembled and nudged him awake.

"An' now, tell them your tale, Wark," Jack urged.

Cheered by food and drink, surrounded by companions, the cobbler essayed forth. The baker, tailor and miller were all held in thrall by the notion of a dragon in their very town, and Wark, as the center of attention, could not resist the opportunity to embellish the previous night's adventure. He brought the story to a rousing finish, ending with the beast staring down at him.

"An' then what?" asked the tailor.

Wark paused for effect. "Th' creature belched..." seeing disappointment in his audience, he quickly added, "...out a flame as like to catch the shutters afire!"

Expressions of surprise and amazement followed, and over a pitcher of ale, Wark and his cronies mused over the incident. None saw the dour churchman who sat listening in a far corner.

Wark returned to his shop for the afternoon and was cutting leather for a pair of boots when he heard his name called loudly followed by a banging on his door.

"Cobbler Wark! Open the door!"

"A moment, a moment," Wark sighed as he crossed

the room. Expecting a customer, he swung wide the door, only to be confronted by the priest, two churchmen and the provost, all with stern countenance.

"Ah, good day--" he began, then was seized by the churchmen, one on each side. The priest began to intone scripture while the provost read from a parchment.

"Citizen Wark, you stand accused of witchcraft and trafficking with the devil, a most heinous crime against the Holy Church." As the provost continued, the priest's recitation became louder until both had raised their voices; a crowd began to gather, adding their muttering to the din.

"You are under arrest and will remain a prisoner until your trial. So sayeth we this day." With that, he nailed the parchment to the cobbler's door, and Wark was led away in stunned silence.

Some consternation ensued since, miscreants in the village being few and far between, there existed no official place of incarceration. After some whispered discussion between priest and provost, they escorted Wark to the miller's root cellar  and locked him in without further ceremony.

Cramped and earthy-smelling, the cellar was dug into the hillside beneath the mill, rather more a tunnel than a structure.  As he grew accustomed to the dark, Wark groped about  and came upon a large pile of flour sacks.  He sat down, sighing, and reflected upon the confusion of the day.

'Twas certain his encounter with the dragon was the cause of it all, granted; rumors had spread from the tavern, he wagered, all the way to the church and back again, each version farther from the truth. "Many's a tale lost in the retelling," he said aloud to himself, settling down on the flour sacks.

Trial, the provost had said. "Trial, humf," Wark muttered. Being paraded through the streets like a tethered ox was trial enough for him. The entire affair had taxed his patience and his dignity past all endurance. There being little else to do, he sat, chin in hand, and waited for his supper.

He dozed off, and was jerked awake by the rattle and scrape as the door was unlocked.

"Master Wark, sir, 'tis I, Jacob, the miller's prentice." In one hand Jacob held a basket, in the other a candle, for night had fallen.

Wark reached for the basket, and the young man whispered hesitantly, "I've..."

Barely had the words escaped his lips when one large hand seized him by the shoulder and yanked him backward. The candle flame vanished, but even in the dark, Wark knew the miller's voice.

"Orders of the provost, Jacob, not to be speakin' to the prisoner." The door was bolted shut, and the cobbler was left standing in the dark holding the basket. He felt his way back to the pile of flour sacks and sat down.

"Prisoner! Not even 'friend Wark' nor 'Wark the cobbler.' Prisoner, indeed," he huffed to himself. Then, hungry, he felt inside the basket: a wooden trencher of boiled turnips, a great chunk of bread, and underneath, a tankard. With optimism Wark dipped one finger into the liquid for a taste.

"Paugh! Water." His initial disappointment began to

fade as he dined; he gave up counting how many turnips he consumed, and the bread was only a mite stale. Belching, Wark drained the tankard, set it back into the basket, and pulled up more flour sacks to cover himself for the night. He found they warmed him enough, and unlike his own grimy bedclothes, were indeed clean. As Wark began to fall asleep, he turned, tugging another sack over his head, and yawned happily, for he felt not a single flea.

The next day being a Thursday with no services observed, the proceedings took place at the church, the inside of which Wark saw all too infrequently. He was sequestered opposite the pulpit, given no place to sit; the provost was present, as was the priest, the two churchmen, and a handful of curious onlookers clustered in the back pews near the door. Clearing his throat, the provost began.

"Cobbler Wark, you are here this day charged as follows: consorting with Satan..."

At mention of that most unholy entity, the friar again commenced his Latin liturgy while he lit several large candles.

"...trafficking with the familiars of the underworld..." The priest began to chant in earnest, which caused the provost to raise his voice, "...and summoning forth Beelzebub, for ungodly deeds and nefarious purposes!" The provost had to fairly shout over the friar's reedy mumbling. At each mention of the devil in any form, he intoned louder and faster, until his frenzied monotone was unintelligible to any present, had they even known Latin. At last they finished simultaneously, the provost out of patience, and the priest out of breath.

"What say you in your defense?" the provost asked Wark.

"If your lordship will recall," Wark began, "I came to you, it's been nigh on two months now, about ridding the town of cats, which as everyone knows is familiars to witches..." There were some gasps from the rear of the church, and the provost pointed a long finger at Wark.

"Mr. Wark, do you practice witchcraft?"

"Which craft? I practices shoe-making, that's my craft," Wark nodded earnestly.

"No, no, man, about the witches..."

"Which is, what, sir? I'm not getting your meaning." Wark cocked his head to one side. Giggling was heard from the back pews.

The provost shook his head and tried another line of inquiry.

"Now, Mr. Wark, confess of the night you invoked the serpent..."

"There wasn't no invoking, m'lord. 'Twas the rats squeaking and scurrying outside my window, so careful as could be, I opened the shutter for a peek out, it being my duty as a responsible citizen." Laughter hooted from the rear of the church.

"Then what were your actions?" the provost asked sternly.

"I did not a thing, sir, but stand an' watch as the creature came from the well: first its head, then its long neck, then its wings folded down flat-like, a long body it had, an' four legs, all up out of the well."

"What was your communion with this creature?"

"Begging your pardon, m'lord, 'twas no creature, 'twas a dragon, plain to see."

Growing exasperated, the provost went on. "What was the nature of your unholy alliance with the serpent?"

"You mean the dragon, sir?"

"No! Yes! Mind you, answer the question!"

"If I take your meaning, I stood and watched it come up the street, then it fixed me with its green eyes, and..."

"And then..."

"...it brought up a belch that near knocked me over!" Wark rubbed the back of his head and looked around sheepishly. "Then I hid in my bed. That's all, m'lord."

Outright guffaws erupted among the spectators, and at least one churchman could be seen suppressing a smirk. The provost banged his fist on the table to restore order, in part to retain his dignity, and in part of keep the priest from chanting again. After a brief whispered conference with the friar, he addressed the gathering.

"Dragons, serpents and devils are all the same in their blasphemy to God. The church finds you must recant your most unholy claims to receive forgiveness. What say you, man?"

"Recant?" Wark echoed, puzzled.

"Admit it, man! Admit these are all lies," the provost pounded the table again for emphasis, "and cleanse your soul!"

Wark was taken aback. A simple man, he unfailingly told the truth mainly because lying required far too much thought.

"Have you naught to say?" the provost demanded.

Wark shrugged, palms outstretched.

"I've but told the truth," he began.

"Take him away!" Impatiently the provost gestured to the churchmen and Wark was escorted back to the root cellar without fanfare.

He ruminated, sitting once again on the pile of flour sacks, not about his immortal soul, but on his untended shop, and not least, his rumbling stomach. Thus he leaped up joyfully at the sound of the door being unbolted.

"It's me, Jacob," the young man furtively glanced over his shoulder as he pulled two apples and a wedge of cheese from his shirt.

Wark gathered the food in his hands eagerly.

"Master Wark, there's..." Jacob began, but the cobbler interrupted.

"Aye, there's a fine lad. Now if you'll but do me one favor, Jacob." The young man nodded.

"You know my shop in town?"

"Aye."

"On the shelf by the door is a pair of boots. They go to the blacksmith--"

"I know him. But...I'll need a key..."

Wark shook his head ruefully. "I had no time to lock up. It's my guess you can walk straight in."

Jacob turned to go, then hesitated. "I have to tell you..."

"It can wait, lad. Go now, and keep a sharp eye." The door closed; Wark heard the scrape and rumble as it was bolted, quick footsteps that faded, then silence. He devoured the first apple, gobbled the cheese, then finished the second apple slowly, savoring its crispness. His meal over, he wiped his hands on his shirt and went back to his pile of flour sacks. It had been a long morning, and Wark decided a nap would set him right.

He woke to a knocking on the door, and heard the miller's voice.

"Wark! Best say your prayers, man. The bishop will be here tomorrow an' he takes not lightly to deviltry from what I've heard," the miller reported woefully. "An' you have my sympathy, friend. Good night."

The bishop. Even when the old woman was accused of bewitching the cow, no one summoned the bishop. That did not bode well, Wark reflected. He lay staring into the musty dark. He had told his neighbors what he had seen, told the provost the truth, and there was naught else to be done. Would they use the ducking stool on him, he wondered? The stock? The pillory? Surely they would not demand he be burned at the stake, or drawn and quartered? With these contemplations, as afternoon darkened into evening, the captive cobbler thus worked himself into such a nervous state that, upon hearing a faint rapping on the door, he sprang up shaking.

"Yiiii!"

"Sh! Sh!" A voice responded over the scratch and thump of the bolt.

Wark hugged both arms around himself. "Whu...whu...who..." he stammered.

With the door opened, the waxing moon shed sufficient light for him to recognize Jacob, just as the young man reached out and grabbed the cobbler's shirt.

"Come now, be quick!" Wark was tugged out of the cellar, downhill and round the side of the mill to the edge of the stream.

"Wait here," Jacob whispered urgently, then made his way to a small boat at the water's edge . "This will do for an escape, aye?"

A glow spread through the cobbler, finer than any ale ever to touch his lips.

He was saved! He was free!

"Get in, keep to the center, and I'll be right after," Jacob instructed, his voice kept low.

"Ah, how can I ever repay you, lad..." Wark's expression of gratitude was cut short as Jacob gave him a gentle shove.

"Mind you don't step on the oars, and sit down!"

Wark inched gingerly to the middle of the boat and sat as he was told. Behind him Jacob eased the boat farther into the water and hopped in, rocking the small craft while the cobbler gripped the wooden edge nervously.

"Take care, Jacob, lest we drown!"

"You've but to stand up, man, 'tis only waist-deep," Jacob chuckled. Mollified, Wark sat in silence as the current slowly carried them downstream, leaving their darkened village behind.

Jacob spoke at last, his voice hushed.

"I know you've not been consorting with the devil," he began.

"Ah, lad 'tis a boon to my soul that you..." Wark exclaimed.

"...an' reason is, I've seen the dragon myself."

Wark could do naught but gasp, half-turning to look at Jacob in amazement.

"I hid down in the grain storage of an afternoon for a bit of rest. Them sacks of grain weigh much as a horse! Well, I fell asleep and waked up to hear a kind of slithering noise..."

"Aye!" Wark slapped his knee, nodding in agreement.

"...an' a bit of squeaking, which waked me right up as I'm not too fond o' rats."

"Nor me."

"'Twas just light enough to see, an' I could tell 'tweren't a snake, nor a weasel neither. Well, like to turned me to stone, I was so struck with fear, I don't mind telling! 'Twas that dragon, sure enough, creeping about, eating them rats right down, bones an' all. " Jacob shuddered.

"When the miller shouted down for me, I was startled out of my wits. I was up the stairs in a trice, lost sight of the dragon, hidden behind the grain sacks as likely." He took a deep breath. "An' that's my tale."

"You never told nobody..."

"Right you are!" Jacob snorted derisively. "To my thinking, if they disbelieved the village cobbler, a sprout prentice was a gone goose! There'd be the both of us in the root cellar, certain!" Guiding the boat along, using his oar as a tiller, he continued.

"I tried to tell you that first night, an' the miller whisked me away. Next when I brought the apples, you sent me off delivering boots--"

"Ah, and were they to the blacksmith's liking?" Wark asked. For all his failings, he had mastered his craft and took not a little pride in his work.

"Oh, aye, he..." Jacob broke off laughing, and Wark turned, curious, to see him slipping off one shoe.

"Gave me a gold crown, he did, said 'twas yours in payment!" With that, Jacob handed the coin to the surprised cobbler.

Wark glanced down at the shoe Jacob had removed. Stitches were parting at the seams, and a small hole in the sole promised to get bigger.

"Needs patching, that one does."

"An' you ought to see the other," Jacob went on. "Now, just on ahead, the stream meets the river, then a bit father there's a village I've heard seems in need of a shoemaker."

"A bright lad you are, Jacob," Wark beamed, pocketing the coin. "Well suited to the cobbler's trade, if I do say so."

"H'mm, no grain sacks to lift..." Jacob reflected philosophically.

"...an' no dragons neither!"

"Aye!" Muffled laughter faded as the small boat disappeared round a bend in the river.

The bishop never did arrive, and in fact suspended all travel until the plague abated. The townsfolk, aghast at Wark's fate, were openly relieved at his escape, while at the tavern, the fabled encounters with the dragon became legendary.

Over the years, it was for those tales the town was eventually renamed: near Stokesly in Yorkshire, it may still be found on old maps, called Dragonswell. It achieved notoriety during one of the plague times for its complete lack of vermin; ironically, according to preserved diaries, in  the village  there was not a cat to be found.

^^^

# CELESTIAL WISDOM

"Mister Scoggins!"

"Aye, Cap'n Pangbourne!" Virtue Scoggins pulled his wool cap down firmly and, rather nimbly for a man his age, climbed down the rope ladder into the small boat. Scoggins did not want to keep the captain waiting. Only a short distance away, the Portuguese galleon sat disabled, rigging torn and sails shredded by cannon fire. She wallowed low in the water, heavily laden with cargo that now belonged to the English crown.

As captain of H.M.S. *Arrow*, Richard Pangbourne served proudly as a privateer of Queen Elizabeth. He wanted it made clear that he seized goods under the auspices of Her Majesty and did not commit robbery like a common pirate. Well-educated, he was fluent in both French and Spanish. However, the subtle nuances of the Portuguese language eluded him, thus he was accompanied by the ship's navigator. The only man aboard who spoke fluent Portuguese was Virtue Scoggins.

The son of a lumber broker in Deptford, young Scoggins had been sent to school in London. A bright lad, he enjoyed learning and excelled in languages. Moreover, he exhibited a flair for penmanship and illuminating which delighted the schoolmasters. A clerk's life seemed his destiny, until the city of London lured him away from his desk, and down to the docks. There he was filled with wonder as he encountered strange cargo, animals from faraway ports, explorers, ship captains, privateers, and once even saw the Queen herself. Scoggins decided that what lay ahead for him was not the life of a merchant. He wanted to learn and see firsthand all the world had to offer. When his studies were accomplished, he signed as an apprentice navigator aboard a privateering vessel.

On his second voyage, the ship captured a French merchant vessel and Scoggins joined the boarding party. Below decks, he spied a swarthy little old man in monk's robes, cowering near the crew's quarters. Upon inquiring he was told the man was a Portuguese prisoner; indignant that they would capture a man of God, he promptly interceded on the monk's behalf. Over protests of the French captain, the old man was brought aboard. The trip back to England was safe and uneventful, and to relieve boredom Scoggins passed time chatting in Latin with the monk. He introduced himself as Fr. Manuel and offered to teach the young navigator Portuguese. Fr. Manuel had been a missionary in China, and told tales of an exotic land where winged serpents dwelled in the Emperor's palace, and people ate unsavory fare such as dog meat and rats boiled in rice. One day as Scoggins made entries on a new map, the monk took the pen and made mysterious ink dribbles on a piece of parchment. Fr. Manuel explained it was the Chinese way of writing, that each word was actually a picture. Scoggins sat wide-eyed, and knew he had made the right decision. Other men could have the gold; knowledge was treasure for Virtue Scoggins.

As they boarded the Portuguese ship, a short stout man identified himself to Captain Pangbourne.

"Captain Antonio del Acaba," Scoggins duly translated.

"Tell him I seize his goods under authorization of Queen Elizabeth of England with whom his sovereign is at war."

Scoggins began to speak but was cut short by Captain del Acaba.

"He knows full well the practices of English pirates." del Acaba cast a look of superiority at Pangbourne, obviously amused that the English captain required an interpreter, and a rather unimpressive-looking one at that. Indeed, with spectacles perched on his nose, graying hair unruly under his cap, and coat overlarge for his thin shoulders, Scoggins did not cut a dashing figure.

"Tell him were we true pirates we would seize his ship and his men, but in the name of Her Majesty we will demand only his cargo."

His animosity tempered with not a little relief, del Acaba agreed to Pangbourne's terms. Formalities thus observed, the crew of the *Arrow* fell to transferring goods from the Portuguese ship. A sizeable cache of wooden chests full of gold coins was hauled up; casks of brandy, more chests, barrels aromatic with coffee and spices followed. Then more exotic plunder appeared: bolts of silken cloth embroidered with golden threads and tiny bright beads, lacquered baskets, ornamental carved wooden boxes.

"What do you make of this, Mr. Wheeler?" Pangbourne asked his first mate.

"A return voyage from Portuguese holdings on the coast, India as likely..."

"Hah! It has been a long trip for them then. We'll lighten their load so as not to overtax their ship, being that she is not altogether seaworthy just at present." Wheeler and the captain laughed as they went belowdecks to supervise.

Scoggins continued to observe the steady flow of cargo. The salt tang of the sea air mingled with the sweet smells of incense from ornate wood boxes as they were carried by. Suddenly Pangbourne's voice boomed from beneath the deck.

"Mister Scoggins!"

"Aye, Cap'n." The navigator descended into the hold, blinking as his eyes adjusted to the darkness.

"Here, man." Matthew Wheeler beckoned from a corner and pointed to a chest the size of a small trunk. It was intricately carved in an open grillwork design, and fastened to its top was a thin metal plate engraved with tiny markings. Wheeler cocked his head to one side.

"Indian writing, d'ye suppose?"

Scoggins inched closer and adjusted his spectacles. "Aye, 'tis writing, but not Indian." He squatted down for a better look. "Chinese, I wager."

Leaning over, he frowned in concentraton."Ah...'heaven'...no,no...'celestial'...yes, that's it..." Scoggins straightened. " 'Celestial Wisdom.' Astronomy writings, as likely."

"Hah!" Captain Pangbourne rubbed his hands together, clearly excited at prospect of securing any navigational assistance. "Take it to my cabin straight away." Wheeler lifted the chest and nearly lost his balance.

"There's scarce any weight to it, sir," he gasped, recovering his footing.

"Have a care there, Matthew," Pangbourne laughed. "Come to my cabin tonight, Scoggins, we'll go over these maps. I daresay we can always do with more wisdom."

That evening as Captain Pangbourne made entries in his journal, he was annoyed by soft squeaking and rustling. "Poxy mice," he muttered. He capped his inkwell and closed the ship's log just as a timid knock came at the door.

"It's Scoggins, sir."

"Yes, come in, man. Let's have a look at these astronomical treasures." Scrutinizing it more closely, they perceived that the chest's design was actually lattice-work, a pattern of small openings, not unlike a small cage. The Captain undid the satiny vermilion cord that secured the brass fastener together; again the rustling noise came, not from mice in the cabin, but from within the chest. Pangbourne lifted the rounded top, and peered inside.

"Almighty God!" Pangbourne slammed the lid shut again and turned to the navigator, eyes wide.

Scoggins had never seen the captain so agitated, short of victory in battle. Indeed, he now brandished his quill pen like a sword, gesturing toward the Chinese chest. Ink flew.

" 'tis an imp of Satan himself, Scoggins, an...an abomination!"

Cautiously Scoggins drew on his spectacles, and listened at the top of the chest. "If you'll permit me, sir?" Carefully he lifted the lid and looked within. Looking back at him were two bright green eyes.

"What it is, is a..."

"What, man, what?"

"A dragon, Captain. Not much more than a hatchling, to judge by its size. You can see, its wings are ..."

" 'ods bodkins, man, shut the chest before it escapes and attacks us!" Pangbourne backed away from the table.

Scoggins suppressed a smile. "It's got no teeth yet, sir." He reached inside and a pigeon-like cooing sound came forth. "I've seen one, many years ago, in Macao. 'Tis strictly forbidden to take them from China. This one was likely a gift from the Emperor to one of his ministers, and captured by the Portuguese."

The navigator gently lifted the small creature out. "Ah, m' beauty. Just a baby, she is," he said, supporting the dragon's body with one hand as he stroked the small wedge-shaped head. Its smooth green skin was the color of oak leaves in spring, tiny scales no bigger than lentils covered its back, and its slim tail twined around Scoggins' arm as he scratched under its chin. With squirrel-like chattering, it craned its long neck upward and spread fragile wings, thin as rose petals.

Scoggins reassured Pangbourne as he approached with trepidation. "No telling how long she's been cooped up in her cage, needs to stretch a bit, she does." Pangbourne moved a bit closer.

"Mind you keep a good hold on the creature, Scoggins." Slowly, holding it by the nib, the captain extended his quill pen. After inspecting it for a moment, the baby dragon suddenly lunged its head forward, seizing the feather end of the pen in its mouth.

"Aye, hi!" Startled, Pangbourne let go of the pen. The dragon held its prize daintily in its front claws, looking satisfied. Scoggins could contain himself no longer and laughed. "Pardon, Cap'n." He pried the pen from the baby dragon's grip and returned it to Pangbourne. "Your pen, sir." Transferring the hatchling to his shoulder, Scoggins reached into the chest.

"Perhaps 'tis merely a tale, but...dragons are the guardians of pearls for the Emperor, so the story goes...ah." Triumphantly, he held out his hand to Pangbourne.

The captain stared. In the navigator's ink-stained palm was a pearl the size of a robin's egg, shimmering in the candlelight.

"God's nightgown, I've never seen such a thing!" Pangbourne took up the pearl and then, as he turned to Scoggins, it was his turn to laugh. The tiny dragon had crept round the navigator's neck and was stealthily staring at the captain, its head protruding from Scoggins' frizz of gray hair.

Retrieving the creature, Scoggins put it gently back into its cage. "Have you some water, sir? I'm thinking she may have a thirst..."

"Ah, to be sure, to be sure." Pangbourne hastily tucked the pearl in a leather pouch on his writing table, then took up his water jug and poured a bit into a clean teacup.

"Back to the brig with you, my fine pen-thief." Scoggins set the cup carefully into the cage and closed the lid. "Would she not make a fine pretty to bring Her Majesty, Cap'n?"

Smiling slightly, Pangbourne crossed his arms. "Not

a word of this to the crew. 'Tis certain they would think we had been pinching the grog."

"Aye, Cap'n," Scoggins agreed, nodding. "Begging your leave, an' good night to you, sir."

The next day H.M.S. *Arrow* anchored in a sheltered cove on the coast. Rigging was adjusted, Scoggins detailed a new map, and the first mate requested permission to take men ashore in search of fresh water.

"Mr. Wheeler!" shouted the captain from the quarterdeck.

"Aye!"

"Take two of the gunnery crew with you and fetch us some meat!"

"Aye, Cap'n!" The men fell to rowing the short distance to shore, lustily singing of pigs, sweet and fat, and women with similar qualities.

It was late in the day when Scoggins took a walk on deck to stretch his legs and relieve his stiff neck. Squinting in the setting sun, he could just make out the smallboat with Wheeler and the men returning to the ship. Then his view was blocked by something very large, and dark.

Scoggins held the telescope to his eye, its brass rim cold on his cheekbone. Steep sides swept upward to sails, tall and spiky as bat's wings. Elaborate latticework adorned the foc'sle, and on the bow, no figurehead - instead, staring out vigilantly at the seas ahead, were two enormous painted eyes.

"By Harry, it's a Chinese junk!" Instantly Captain Pangbourne was at his side. "Here, Cap'n, have look."

# TEN DRAGON TAILS

Pangbourne seized the telescope.

"Is it pirates or a merchant vessel, Scoggins?"

"Can't make it out, Cap'n..."

"Wait now...God's teeth, now there's two!" He thrust the telescope back to the navigator.

"Aye, off to starboard..." Scoggins fell quiet. "Getting on dark soon, Cap'n..."

He paused, then continued. "Wheeler and the men...they're nowhere to be seen, sir."

As twilight deepened, eerie quiet enveloped the HMS *Arrow*. Pangbourne and Scoggins stood gripping the quarterdeck railing and staring out into the blackness beyond their ship. Suddenly a tiny speck of light flared in the distance, firefly-quick; then another, then more and more, which became glowing spheres as they came closer and closer. Lanterns, scores of them, reflected a golden-brown light in the water below as the Chinese junks neared.

A shout went up from one of the Chinese boats. Scoggins strained to hear, then turned to Captain Pangbourne, his voice kept low.

"They are representatives of the Emperor... They say they know we have Celestial Wisdom... Its return is the ransom... for release of our men."

"Yes, man, of course tell them yes," Pangbourne replied immediately, nodding, never once taking his eyes off the lantern-lit ships. Scoggins shouted a reply, then hurried below to fetched the chest from the Captain's cabin.

The men appeared out of the night, rowing for all they were worth under escort of two small Chinese boats, lit fore and aft with tall, swaying lanterns. The navigator bowed to the Chinese spokesman, who stared at him, then bowed in return. As he took the chest, he replied to Scoggins, then climbed into one of the small boats. Yellow lanterns bobbed and danced, becoming smaller as they returned to the Chinese junks.

Wheeler and the men were giddy with relief, all talking at once of strange things they had witnessed on board the junk.

"They stared at us, poked us a bit..."

"Laughed at us, they did..."

"What was in that chest, Cap'n?"

Pangbourne hesitated, then cleared his throat. "Ah...the Chinese take their astrology very seriously, it would appear..."

"Well an' it's a good thing for us. You rescued us none too soon, as was dinner-time on their ship an' it appeared none too tasty."

"Fish, I'll wager," replied Captain Pangbourne.

"Worst yet, this great fat Chinese ran round with a cleaver and was slicing rats to put in the stew!"

Captain Pangbourne made a retching noise, and the men jeered.

Later, in the Captain's cabin, Scoggins sighed over his rum. " 'Twould have been grand to fetch back a dragon for Her Majesty."

"Aye." Pangbourne nodded in agreement. "Now there's a thing neither Francis Drake nor Dandy Jack Hawkins ever brought from the New World." Suddenly the Captain pounded his fist on the table.

"Hah!" He jumped up and rummaged over his desk

until he found the leather pouch containing the pearl. "Let it not  be said we returned empty-handed, man!" he beamed, lifting his tankard triumphantly. "By the way, what did that Chinese  say to you, Scoggins?"

"He was amazed that a barbarian pirate speaks the language of the Middle Kingdom."

"Hmm. Indeed." Pangbourne took another drink. "Scoggins?"

"Yes, sir?"

"Do the Chinese really eat rats?"

"Yes, sir, boiled with rice."

Pangbourne shuddered. "Dragons in the hold, rats in the rice, 'sblood but they are a heathen lot!"

Scoggins peered over the tops of his spectacles. "Aye, Cap'n, but they do possess Celestial Wisdom." Laughter was heard on deck from the Captain's cabin, and the men wagered he was pinching the grog.

Richard Pangbourne presented Queen Elizabeth with the pearl of Celestial Wisdom and received a privateer's pension. Virtue Scoggins was appointed Royal Mapmaker, his finely detailed work prized for its accuracy. Embellished with intricate designs, every map bore his trademark: in flowing script, in the seas off China, were the words: 'Here Be Dragons.'

∧∧∧

# IRINOVA REMEMBERS

Cousin Drushka was old, and cousin Irinova was even older. At eighty-five, Irinova's hearing was not the best and her joints were beginning to stiffen, but her voice remained that of a young woman, clear and lilting. When she began one of her stories, all the little ones would gather near to listen. She spun out long fairy tales, of Baba Yaga the witch; leshiye, the mischievous spirits that waylaid travelers in the woods; of vyrkalak, the evil ones that drank men's blood; of rusalka, the water-nymphs; and best of all, the dragons, wily, strong, and mysterious. When the young cousins were sufficiently mesmerized and sent to bed, she and Drushka would share their own tales: village gossip and scandalous revelations about family members. This they did one afternoon in late summer.

At the parlor window, Irinova opened the shutters just as Drushka entered with the tea tray.

"It is so gray and humid today," Irinova sighed. "The air is still and heavy, Drushka, there will be a storm later."

"Tsk, how you can predict the weather just by standing at the window," Drushka teased. "Come and have tea." Drushka had cared for Irinova since the accident; a shy, clumsy girl, she never married, but instead became a capable companion to her beloved cousin.

Irinova made her way to her chair just as Drushka placed a tall glass of hot tea in her hand. "It is a talent I have perfected," she replied wryly, settling herself.

"The cows and goats are restless all through the village, Irinova. The dogs are pacing about, sniffing the air..."

"It is the storm coming. They sense the excitement." Irinova raised her shoulders. "Can you not feel it? Do you know, Drushka, it was a day as this, just such a day..."

At sixteen, Irinova was much like the butterflies she chased: quiet, beautiful, quick and elusive. Once her daily chores were finished, she gave a brief word to her father at his workbench, then went to the forest. It was but a short journey for young legs, and there Irinova made wildflower garlands, fed the squirrels, or gathered wild mint by the stream. But more often than not, she sat leaning against a tree reading, for books were her great passion.

She was thus occupied one spring afternoon, when the sound of cautious crackling and rustling made her stiffen with apprehension; there were deer and rabbits in the woods, but also bears. To her relief, the noise ceased. Then, two days after, as she chased a big yellow butterfly along the stream, she tripped on a tree root and fell with a thump.

"Ooof!" Unhurt, Irinova brushed leaves from her blouse. "A good thing no one saw," she muttered to herself, but as she got to her feet she heard what sounded like laughter.

"Come out where I can see you!" she called out. Then the crunching of footsteps faded into quiet once more. "Humf." Too indignant to be afraid, she shook the leaves from her skirt and marched home, dusty and red-faced.

The next day she paused from reading to get a drink from the stream. As she bent to cup her hands in the cold water, she caught her breath, for kneeling in the tall grass on the opposite bank, very still like a deer catching a scent, was a young man. Irinova sat up straight and faced him.

"I see you." She balled her hands into fists so he could not see them shaking. "You do not frighten me."

"I did not attempt to," he replied calmly.

Irinova scrambled to her feet but when she looked across the stream, he was gone. She resumed reading that afternoon, but with difficulty, recalling that he was rather handsome.

The very next day she took not only a book to read, but a good-sized basket as well, and sang to herself the whole way. She chose a shady place under an oak tree, put down the basket, and took out a linen cloth. She spread it out on the ground, then sat quietly listening until, alerted at soft crunching sounds, she spoke out loudly.

"I'm getting very hungry. If you don't come sit down this instant, I'm going to gobble up all the food here and you will have none." Irinova paused, then heard a soft laugh. He appeared from behind a thicket and approached her, carrying a bouquet of wildflowers. Taking off his cap with one hand, he offered her the flowers with the other.

"Oh!" Irinova reached up and took the flowers

graciously. "Are these for me? But how did you know I would be here?"

He gestured at the cloth and basket. "The same way you knew I would join you for tea." He made a short bow and took her hand. "I am Sascha Petrovich."

"I am Irinova Razinskaya. Please be seated."

Sascha sat opposite her, tailor-fashion. "Are you really as hungry as you said?" he asked.

"Yes!" Irinova began unpacking the basket. "I have bread, cheese, here are some cold dumplings, a few strawberries, and a jug of tea."

"You brought tea?" Sascha leaned forward, clearly pleased.

"Here, these cups are chipped, but they will do." While she talked, Irinova uncorked the jug and poured tea for both of them. "I'm afraid it is not very hot."

Sascha sipped, then closed his eyes and sighed. "It is excellent. "

Though in truth Irinova was hungry, apparently Sascha, who ate politely but without stopping, was much more so. She watched him over her chipped teacup, taking in his appearance: the tunic, coat and cap, all shabby and faded, the holes in his trousers, the worn boots wrapped with strips of leather. He was fascinating.

"Thank you, Irinova Razinskaya, for that most excellent meal." Not a scrap of food remained.

"You are most welcome." Irinova blushed.

"You are quite the bold one, coming to the woods alone."

Irinova shrugged. "The forest has a quiet beauty. I

have spent many afternoons here in summers. I feel safe now, but not when I was a child..."

"You are still a child," he laughed.

"I am sixteen," she said indignantly.

"Oh, I beg your pardon, milady," Sascha laughed. "Was it the bears and wolves you feared?"

"Oh, no!" Irinova leaned forward, serious and wide-eyed. "It was the leshiye, and the vyrkalak..."

Sascha rolled his eyes and groaned.

"...but most of all, the dragon they say lives here on the mountain!"

Sascha laughed, shaking his head. "You are still a child, then! Those are stories for children."

"You may laugh, but my father still speaks of the evil things here." Irinova crossed her arms.

"Does he not worry about you, then? And your mother..."

"My mother is dead," Irinova replied curtly. She began gathering up cups and linen, packing them into the basket. "My father is a master woodcarver in the village and is always busy with his work. He scarcely knows I am gone." She brushed a wisp of hair from her eyes. "What work do you do, Sascha Petrovich?"

"Whatever I can find," he shrugged. "I manage."

"You live in the village, then?"

"No. Here." Sascha spread out his hands.

"Here in the woods? You're joking, there is no house-"

"That means no house to clean, no beds to make, no hearth to sweep."

Irinova raised her eyebrows. "So..." she said slowly,

"...have you ever seen the dragon?"

"You are persistent, Irinova." Sascha sniffed impatiently as he helped her up. "There are evils to deal with in life, more important than your dragon." Reaching down for the basket, he handed it to her and touched his cap. "I regret I cannot see you to your door." He smiled at her, turned, and had gone but a few paces when he disappeared into the trees.

"He really disappeared?" Drushka pressed on, intrigued.

"Tcha! I mean only that he knew those woods that well, so that every tree, every rock, every blade of grass was as familiar to him as your hearth is to you."

"Oh." Drushka sat quietly, somewhat let down. Then she brightened. "Was he handsome?"

"Aha!" Irinova ducked her head between her shoulders, blushing. "That I can remember! He had blue eyes, not light blue, but lapis blue, very mischievous, and when he smiled, one side of his mouth turned up more than the other.

"And his hair was brown, light brown, when his cap was off he ran his fingers through it when he talked, and Drushka, his voice was so very pleasant, so friendly, it made me feel I had known him always."

"Was he tall?"

"Only just taller than I. He had but a short beard..."

"Ah, he was young..."

"Yes... but there were moments when I saw him set

his jaw, saw his eyes go darker and heard his voice harden, when he appeared to be much, much older...."

Sascha's presence in the woods was not to be predicted; some days he was there, others passed with no sign of him. Irinova read her book or ate her food by herself then, reasoning that she had, after all, come there to be alone. Late one afternoon she was reading when she heard quiet footsteps nearby and held her breath; it could be a deer, or it could be...

"Sascha?" she called timidly, then jumped, startled, as he knelt beside her. "Sascha, you gave me a fright! You pass about so, like a wraith, I think you are *leshiye*!"

"I am no forest spirit that plays tricks on you. So-- is that what you are reading, more fairy tales?" As he sat down, he turned the book to read its title and smiled. "Ah, poetry."

"You can read?" Irinova blurted.

Sascha leaned back and tipped his cap over his eyes. "My mother taught me when I was a boy. She insisted her son learn to read and write, although what good she imagined it would do the son of serfs, I cannot say."

Irinova put down the book as he continued.

"Up at dawn to eat gruel, work like an animal all day, come home to meager supper and go to bed: that life leaves no time for books. Ha! There was no place to put any, had we owned them!" He sat up and counted on his fingers. "We had no cupboards, no mirrors, not a pewter candlestick or a brass button. But still the boyars taxed us..." Sascha took off his hat and ran his fingers through his hair.

"They sent hirelings on horseback to enforce their decrees. We had an ox, one tired old ox - and they demanded it! My father tried to tell them we needed the animal to work the land, for our very survival. They ignored him, pushed him aside and seized the ox's halter."

Sascha's eyes flashed, dark and furious, and he struck the ground with his fist. "Never have I known such white-hot anger, Irinova! I stepped in front of the ox, and told them to leave us alone, I called the boyars leeches..."

"Oh!" Irinova's hand went to her mouth in shock.

"...sucking the life from their serfs. My mother began to wail, and my father put his arms around her - then one of the mercenaries swung down and struck me with a club." He stopped and took a deep breath. "I woke up laying in the road with blood in my eyes. It was very cold...the ox was gone..."

Impulsively Irinova reached out and touched his arm. "Oh, Sascha..."

"My father secretly sent my mother to live with her sister. It was only us two..." he paused, his voice lower. "My father died trying to plow our fields by himself. His life is in the land of Russia."

Irinova watched him: his strong hands gripped tight together, muscles in his jaw moving, his expression cold and distant, the scar still white over one eye.

"But, could you not go..."

"I did go. One night I bundled up everything I owned and fled. This -- " he waved his hand, "is where I stopped." His face had lost its hardened look. He got to his feet, took her hand and kissed it.

Irinova blushed. "It is late now, I should return..." Still holding her hand, he helped her up.

"I look forward to seeing you."

She turned to go, then looked back; this time he did not vanish into the trees, but waved and stood watching her.

On her next visit Irinova filled a basket with sweet rolls and books; Sascha was plainly delighted and the pair sat beneath the trees reading and stuffing themselves.

"I believe, Irinova," Sascha began, licking the sugar from his fingers, "that a man can eat too much and drink too much, but he can never learn too much. Every book can teach you something!"

"You may borrow any book of mine that you wish, only please take care, out here --" she looked around anxiously.

"Ah, Irinova, do you think I live in a tree!" Sascha exclaimed. He laughed as he jumped to his feet and grabbed her hand. "Come, come!" He began pulling her after him up the mountain in a zigzag route.

"How much farther?" Irinova panted, out of breath.

"Just ahead." At its steepest, the path turned in sharply: between two gigantic boulders was an opening.

Sascha slipped inside and guided Irinova into the darkness. "Wait here," he instructed, laughter in his voice. Then he struck a match and lit several candles. "This is my home," he said proudly, with a wide sweep of his arm.

Irinova gazed all around. The meager candlelight was

magnified by pieces of broken mirror which Sascha had placed about. She was in a cave, tall enough to stand at the entry, tapering lower toward the rear; in front of her, a circle of stones provided a rough hearth where several cooking pots rested. A tiny cupboard sat against one wall, and opposite it a small stool sat beside a low table, its missing leg propped up with stones. Farthest back, where the light grew dim, folded quilts and blankets lay across an immense nest of evergreen branches.

Sascha stood in front of her, arms crossed, clearly pleased. "I think your books will be safe in here," he said with a roguish smile.

"It is quite charming, Sascha!" Irinova clasped her hands under her chin. "Did you bring all this with you?"

"Scarcely," he scoffed. "Cooking pots, quilts, and the clothes on my back were all I could carry, not that we owned anything else."

"Then where -- "

"It is surprising what the rich discard for the ragman, is it not?"

"How long have you lived here?"

"Three years, this year at harvest time."

"Is it not terribly cold in winter?"

Sascha shrugged. "Outside in the snow, yes. You would be pleasantly surprised at how warm it can be here inside, once the fire is kindled. I have some furs for my bed as well..."

"And food, what do you eat?"

"Rabbit, fowl, sometimes fish. When it is scarce I go to the open market in the village."

"What do you buy?"

"Buy?" Sascha laughed. "I buy nothing. I steal whatever I can."

Scandalized, Irinova giggled. "Sascha, you are a scoundrel!"

He shrugged. "Better to survive as a scoundrel, than starve as a saint. Now, do not look so disapproving, Irinova, I do work sometimes. Cutting wood and tending horses at the tavern earns me a few kopecks, then I come back to the mountain. I have no use for those people."

Irinova shook her head in wonder, then a jolt of anxiety made her gasp. "It is late! I must get home, Father will be displeased..."

Sascha put out the candles and took her hand. "Hmf. You are such a trouble, Irinova Razinskaya, all I do is take you up and down this mountain." They both laughed, racing along the narrow path, birds scattering from trees as they rushed by, all the way to the bottom.

Thereafter, two and sometimes three days a week, Irinova rose at dawn, finished her daily tasks, and went to the forest, returning in the afternoon in time to begin dinner. One day she arrived later than usual and found her father waiting, a deep frown across his brow.

"You spend too much time off in the forest, daughter," he began.

"I am sorry I worried you, Father. I go only when my morning chores are finished, and take with me some food and a book to read. Do not worry, the *leshiye* will not capture me." She looked up at him with a tiny smile that vanished with his reply.

"I do not talk of fairy spirits!" he continued angrily. "Do you not remember the goatherd who went into the forest and never returned? Do you?"

Trembling, Irinova shook her head. "I do not," she answered softly.

"There is real danger on the mountain, daughter. Conduct yourself with care." He said no more, but tidied up his workshop for the night.

Irinova cooked supper and they ate in silence; for the next two days she remained at home.

On the third day, her morning work done, she approached her father at his workbench.

"May I go out today?" she asked solemnly.

He did not look up from his carving. "Go, then, but be watchful."

With a sigh of "Thank you," Irinova was out the door like a caged bird, once again free to fly. She was sitting by the stream, shoes and stockings off, toes in the cool water, when Sascha found her.

"Would you like a plum?" he asked as he sat beside her. "I see you do not jump when I approach now."

"You do not try to be so quiet as before," she replied. "Where did you get the plums?" Indeed he had a hatful of ripe purple fruit.

"Off a tree," Sascha laughed as he tossed one to her. "It may have belonged to someone but I did not stay to ask."

Irinova bit into her plum, giggling as juice ran down her chin. She remembered stealing plums from neighbors' trees with her cousins when they were younger; somehow it made the fruit all the sweeter.

"I missed you," Sascha said matter-of-factly.

"My father was upset that I come here...he told me of a goatherder who vanished, not long ago..." Irinova stopped then, shocked by Sascha's sudden laughter.

"Ah yes, the missing herdsman. Let me tell you the story, Irinova. The poor man owed taxes such that his goats were to be taken and sold, leaving him with no income. Now what is the sense of that? The rich are not only cruel, they are stupid!" Sascha spat out a plum pit for emphasis.

"So one day he was on the mountain with his goats when I happened along and we fell to talking. I devised a way to help him."

"Go on," Irinova urged.

"Days went by, until one morning I found two freshly-killed goats on the hillside. I took him there, wiped his hat and cloak with the blood, and left them with the carcasses. I suggested he leave a shoe as well, but he refused, needing them both to travel. And so he vanished, outwitting the boyars!" Sascha chuckled at the memory.

"But you killed those poor goats!"

"No." Sascha shook his head "I did not kill them. They were already dead when I found them, torn to pieces by a bear."

"Or...it could have been the dragon!" Irinova's eyes widened.

Sascha made a sputtering noise.

"Do you not believe in the legends of the woods---" she went on.

"Ah, Irinova!" Sascha interrupted, exasperated.

"Those are tales the elders tell, to entrance us into forgetting our wretched lives, or to terrify us into behaving. The mountain has dangers all its own, but they befall careless travelers. They are real, not fantasies."

The plums eaten, both Sascha and Irinova washed their sticky hands and faces at the stream, then leaned back on the soft grass. Sunlight through the trees overhead dappled the ground with tiny golden patches.

"The sunshine looks to me like so many coins scattered about," Irinova sighed. "If this were all gold, real gold, Sascha, what would you buy?"

He sat up and ran his palm along the ground as though scooping up money. "I will tell you: I would buy a fine suit of clothes, and new boots, and then I would purchase the most finely-crafted boat I could find. With it I would travel down the water-road to all the great cities of Russia, all the way to the sea. Oh! And I would buy you books, enough to fill your house, so many that it would take you a lifetime to read them all."

"Can you sail a boat?" Irinova asked, leaning upon one elbow.

"No, but I can learn." Sascha set his jaw in determination.

Looking at him, Irinova felt that it would certainly be so. "Tomorrow I will bring us books to read, while we wait for this wealth to come." She took his hand and gave it a squeeze, then got up, brushing off her skirt. "Now I must go, to remain in Father's good graces." She turned to go and had taken but two steps when Sascha called out.

"Irinova!"

"Yes?"

"Have you any books on sailing?" His laughter faded as she followed the path down the hill.

But she did not return the next day, nor the next, nor the day after that, which was a Sunday. It was midday on Monday and hot under the summer sun, when she again went to the forest. Her apron pockets were stuffed with blintzes, a stack of books, bound with an old belt, was tucked under one arm, and Irinova was deep in thought. Sascha did startle her that day.

"Where have you been?" he asked, as he stepped from behind a pine tree.

"Aaah!" Irinova jumped, one hand to her throat. "Sascha, you gave me a fright." She leaned against the tree with a sigh.

"Here, let me take these." Sascha shouldered the books. "I was beginning to worry that you were ill, when you did not come for so many days."

"Father would not let me..."

"Ah, Irinova, in trouble again..." he grinned.

"No, Sascha, he is worried of...have you not been to the village?"

"No, not for days." Sascha shook his head. "Why?"

"It is all the talk, let me tell you! Three nights past, dogs fell to barking all over the village, and next morning many sheep were missing and blood was all over." Irinova paused for breath, then went on excitedly. "And so, night before last, one of the local boys went to fetch his family cow from grazing and heard it bellowing; he ran out toward the forest and saw the poor cow being dragged into the woods, by something, what he could not say, but it was every bit as big as the cow itself."

"A bear could easily bring down a cow..."

"Everyone says it is the dragon...even my father. That is why I was not allowed out of the village."

Sascha gave a disgusted snort. "There are no dragons, Irinova, nor leshiye nor rusalka, nor vampires. The only creatures that drink up our lifesblood are the rich and the royalty." He took her hand firmly. "Come, we will go where it is cool and look over these books."

Just inside the cave entrance, with ample sunlight by which to read, the two of them spread a quilt on the bare earth. It was cool as Sascha predicted, and they lay in comfort munching on blintzes.

"Oh!" Irinova sat upright.

"What is wrong, did a bee sting you?" Sascha was startled.

"No, only I just remembered..." Licking her fingers, she opened the biggest book and took a folded paper from inside the cover. "I've brought you something." She extended the paper to Sascha."Here."

"For me?" Sascha took the paper, clearly excited, and unfolded it. "What is this..."

"It's a map, Sascha, for you to use when you sail down the water road."

Fascinated, he laid the paper flat on the quilt and traced the lines of the rivers with one finger. "Ah, Irinova, this is most marvelous...look, see how easily one can go, all the way to the sea..."

She brushed her hair away from her face as she leaned down next to him. He turned to her then, and taking her face gently between his hands, kissed her softly.

"You are as kind as you are beautiful, Irinova Razinskaya." As he whispered to her, his lips tickled her ear and she began to giggle in spite of herself.

"Oh, you mock me, do you?" Sascha began to laugh as well, tickling Irinova until they both were tousled and breathless. "What is this?" he asked, touching a golden chain around her neck. "I have never seen it before."

Irinova reached behind her neck, undid the clasp, and lay a necklace on the quilt. Four glittering garnet beads, two on each side, complemented a garnet pendant.

"It is as beautiful as you, and that is the truth," Sascha told her.

"I believe it was my mother's," Irinova said quietly as she straightened her hair. "I wear it very seldom, as it seems to upset my father."

Sascha sat back, his arms crossed on one knee. "Perhaps you resemble her..." he began.

Irinova frowned and looked off into the distance. "No, it is because he begrudges me my life. You see, Sascha," she went on, her voice flat with bitterness, "my mother died when I was born. My father was robbed of the young bride whom he worshipped, and left with a baby daughter, hardly a fair trade. Oh, he does not mistreat me -- I am housed and fed, the common courtesies one bestows upon a dog, but Father does not love me. That is part of my life, I accept it."

Sascha put his arms around her and kissed her cheek.

## TEN DRAGON TAILS

"I love you, Irinova, to me you are more precious than all the garnets and gold in the world." He sat for a long while, with her in his arms, rocking her back and forth the way one would an unhappy child. At length, seeing the afternoon shadows changing outside, he sighed and released her. "You must return early today, we cannot have the village thinking you were eaten by the dragon or turned to stone, or..."

Irinova gave him a sharp jab in the side. "Scoff then, my superstitious aunts have hung so many herbs about the front door, the house looks like a haystack." Sascha laughed as he helped her to her feet. She fussed about suddenly, arranging the books on the small table.

"Leave them, I will keep them safe for you." He placed his hands on her shoulders and kissed her again. "Go now."

Irinova ran out, laughing; she turned to wave at Sascha as he stood outlined against the cave's dark interior, then hurried down the mountain.


"It was the next day, Drushka: gray and still, well into the morning, just as now. I had not slept for being so warm, and woke to hear Father talking to some other men. More sheep were missing, and they were planning a search on the mountain, bringing hunting dogs! I knew I must warn Sascha, for if they found him they would take him for a thief or worse. Quickly I dressed and hurried through my morning chores, then called out to Father that I was going out, 'on an errand,' I told him. 'Do not go far, it may rain' was all he said; he was busy at his workbench and did not even look up as I slipped out the door."

"The air was sticky, not a breath of breeze, and there was strange quiet all along the way I took to the forest. But then as I began up the hill, I heard a noise."

"Were you not afraid?"

Irinova paused.

"Do you know, Drushka, I was not. I assumed it was..."

"Sascha, spying on me again," Irinova said aloud to herself. The heavy, thrashing sound was some distance away.

"He will be easy to outwit, the whole forest can hear him." She zigzagged on the now-familiar pathways and paused in a thicket near a dead old oak tree, kneeling down to conceal herself. She held her breath as she heard heavy footfalls approach, then stop; sounds of breathing and moving about gradually faded off into silence. Slowly Irinova raised her head above dense branches.

"Ha, Sascha is not so smart," she laughed softly, looking up the hillside behind her; though steep, it was a shortcut by which she could reach the cave before Sascha. She clambered up, avoiding scrubby thorn bushes and rocks, and reached the top dirty but smug. Irinova wondered what Sascha would say when he came up the hill to find her already there. She had barely sat down at the entrance to the cave, out of breath, when a voice behind her said,

"Irinova? Is that you?"

"Yeek!" She leaped to her feet, hands clutching her wadded-up skirt as she turned and bumped into Sascha, who stood, startled, behind her.

"What, Irinova? What is it?" He grasped her hands firmly.

"You! You frightened me, I was waiting for you, I heard you..."

"Heard me? Where?"

"There was...I came up the mountain to warn you and I heard footsteps, I thought it was you spying on me so I wanted to have joke on you..."

"I have not left the cave all morning. Irinova-- you're shaking." He put both arms protectively around her.

"I heard behind me more footsteps, and someone breathing -- so I came up the short way, to trick you, but if it was not you..." His embrace tightened; she felt the strength of the muscles across his back and smelled woodsmoke in his hair.

Sascha looked down at her, wiped a smudge of dirt from her cheek and impulsively kissed her forehead.

"You are brave as well as bold, Irinova Razinskaya. Now come and sit."

"Have you any tea?" Her voice was muffled against his shirt.

"No," Sascha shook his head. "I must remember to steal some the next time I visit the marketplace." As Irinova laughed, he held her at arms' length.

"You came to warn me, you said?" Sascha asked.

"Oh! Yes!" She leaned forward earnestly. "Men from the village are coming up the mountain with dogs today, to find..."

"Bears?"

"...or the dragon!"

"Aaah!" Sascha pulled at his hair in mock annoyance. "There is no dragon! What must you see to convince you..."

Irinova stuck out her chin defiantly. "What must you see to convince you that there is?"

"The dragon itself! Wings, scales and all..."

"It is settled then, come with me, I will show you where I heard something moving, and if we find so much as one dragon scale, you will admit you are wrong."

"It is a bargain." Together they left the cave. Outside the sky was a thick gray quilt that hung motionless over them as Irinova led Sascha down the mountain, to the thicket near the dead tree.

"Here, it was here I heard it loudest," Irinova called.

"Show me."

She gestured downhill toward a clump of bushes."Dragons," Sascha snorted, and stomped off in the direction where Irinova pointed. He sidestepped thicker bushes and trampled others, until he peered past a jumble of branches and vines to another clearing.

"Aha!" he said in a low voice."Irinova, come here."

Yanking her skirt free from brambles, she made her way over to him. "Look through here, between those two trees, and tell me what you see." He bent and pointed.

"I see..."

"Yes?"

"...something very big and brown."

"Ha!" he whispered jubilantly. "Ha! A bear! As I thought all along!"

"Are you sure?"

"I am going closer for a better look."

"Oh, Sascha, don't..."

"I will be careful. Stay here." Sascha moved silently off toward the clearing, then stopped still, as the gray sky rumbled overhead.

"Oh..." Irinova covered her mouth and held her breath. No sound, no movement came; yet suddenly she decided it was safer with Sascha. Moving in his direction, she stepped on a dry branch that broke with a loud crack. Paralyzed, she stood motionless, her eyes on the wide brown hulk in the clearing, until with a stern look, Sascha motioned her to come forward. The soft grass underfoot made no sound as she joined him.

"Has it moved?" she whispered.

"No...it is very strange." Slowly Sascha stooped down, picked up a rock, and threw it to the far side of the clearing where it landed on a pile of leaves.

The shape remained still. Sascha retrieved a second rock and threw it nearer yet.

"Did he move?"

"No."

The next rock Sascha aimed carefully and threw right at the middle of the brown hulk, where it struck with a soft thump; the thing remained motionless. Sascha motioned for Irinova to remain, as he crept close enough to touch the bulky fur, then made his way around for a better look.

The stink of blood came at him the instant before he saw the carcass as it leaned against the tree. Only the upper jaw and the eyes remained of its head; from the lower jaw the bear was ripped completely open. Flesh hung raggedly and great gobs of blood clotted thick on its torn fur, and over all flies swarmed solid black. The ground felt spongy with blood; scraps of bone and entrails lay at Sascha's feet, and the flies' feverish hum made his skin crawl. Just as a flash of lightning illuminated the clearing, he turned and found himself face to face with Irinova. Though he tried to block her view, she craned her neck past him to see, and just as she began to scream a great clap of thunder shook the whole mountain. Irinova buried her face in Sascha's tunic, not crying but moaning in terror, shaking as she clung to him.

A second flash of lightning snapped across the sky, followed by the boom of thunder. As Irinova screamed again, Sascha held her tightly, then he took her face firmly in his hands.

"Irinova! Come, we are leaving this place, do you understand?" She nodded, eyes filled with tears. "See, it is beginning to rain." He glanced upward and lifted her chin with one hand, then turned her around and guided her firmly from the clearing. It was indeed raining, not a fine drizzle but fat drops that plopped to the ground like pebbles.

"This way, now." Sascha took hold of Irinova's hand and led her downhill, following the stream as it flowed into a ravine with steep sides. Growing canopy-like on an overhang, a massive oak tree provided shelter from the rain. "We will be dry and safe here until the rain stops." Sascha sat cross-legged on the dry ground and pulled Irinova down beside him.

Without hesitating, she leaned against him, her arm

around his neck.

"I have never seen anything so terrible...oh!" Irinova flinched as lightning flashed again, out in the forest. "I am sorry, Sascha, lightning does not always frighten me..."

"You have seen enough this day to frighten anyone." He hugged her close as thunder rumbled, muted and distant. "Listen... it is farther away now. The storm will be over soon."

"Sascha..." Irinova pulled away and took a deep breath."What could kill a bear so?"

He shook his head slowly. "Nothing that I have ever seen."

They sat huddled together in silence as the storm moved on. Gradually the rain stopped, leaving the forest wet and dripping.

"We can return to the cave this way." Sascha got up, stretching, and took her hand. They made their way along the side of the hill, upward, between trees and rocks, slipping on wet leaves, until Irinova stopped.

"What was that?" She pulled at Sascha's arm.

"What?" He looked back at her, puzzled.

"I heard something..." At that moment Sascha heard it too, something of a hiss mixed with a roar, coming from below them. Where they stood, the slope leveled off and became a flat, a rocky ledge, and beyond it was a sheer drop down to the ravine.

Letting go of Irinova's hand, Sascha inched closer to the edge, then lay flat on his stomach for a better view. Irinova crept up beside him, and together they peered down. It was there, just below them, green-bronze as a statue, and as motionless.

"Holy Mother of Saint Gregory!" Sascha whispered.

"It is real, Sascha, it is real, I knew it!" Irinova breathed excitedly.

"I must apologize to you, Irinova Razinskaya. There is indeed a dragon in the forest."

"There really was a dragon?" Drushka leaned forward, intrigued. Just then lightning flickered outside. She flinched and held Irinova's hand.

"Ah, the storm is here, yes?" Irinova patted Drushka's arm reassuringly.

"Why did you never tell me of the dragon?"

"At first, it was because I knew no one would believe me. They would say I was crazed after all I had been through. But then..."

"Yes?" Drushka prompted.

"I decided to keep it to myself, as one keeps a treasure." Thunder pounded outside and the two cousins hugged and laughed.

"Then what--"

The size of a horse, the dragon was covered in leaf-green scales that turned to a metallic, coppery hue on its head and legs, the same color as the ridges down the length of its spine. It sat back on muscular haunches, leathery green wings loosely folded along its back; scales on its neck seemed to sparkle as it twisted this way and that, surveying the ravine.

"It is so magnificent...and so terrible," Irinova

breathed.

"The bear fought for its life," Sascha whispered.
"See, Irinova, the bite wounds its on neck and the deep scratches across its sides, and look -- one of its forelegs is badly mangled."

The dragon had truly paid a price for its kill; blood trickled from cuts and punctures and stained its green scales crimson. The bear had nearly severed one of the dragon's front feet and it hung bleeding and useless, leaving the great beast to move along on its hind legs alone. Irinova did not answer, but lay in mute fascination, watching the fabulous creature; Sascha had to pull twice at her hand to get her attention. He put his finger to his lips and motioned her to follow him, and she did so only with slow reluctance. Carefully they retreated, picking their way around rocks, between trees, up the steep slope toward the safety of the cave. They were nearly there when they heard the roaring hiss again, followed by thrashing sounds coming closer and closer.

"We are almost there, Irinova," Sascha panted. "See, there are the boulders at the cave's entrance." He looked over his shoulder and saw with dismay that she had lagged behind. Impatiently, he waited for her to catch up and held onto her hand.

"Sascha...can we not stop...just for a moment..." Out of breath, she tugged at his arm. Just then amidst the shaking of bushes, the dragon appeared, making its way steadily up toward them.

"That is your answer," Sascha grunted, pulling her after him.

"Sascha... I hear dogs."

"Are you sure it is not the dragon?" he answered between breaths. Then he too heard the baying of hounds, along with the shouts of men.

Below, the dragon heard them as well, and stopped, craning its neck in apprehension. Sascha lost no time in hauling Irinova up the slope, and pushed her ahead of him up onto the flat ledge in front of the cave.

"Stand back," Sascha began breathlessly. As he began to climb over, his hands slipped on the muddy ground and he lost his footing on the wet leaves, sliding back down the hillside until his foot lodged against an oak sapling. The sounds of the dogs grew nearer; he looked over his shoulder for the dragon but it was nowhere in sight. Scrambling, grabbing at rocks and branches, he worked his way back up the steep hill. This time he climbed up a rockfall just a few paces farther to his left, which brought him right upon the path, just around a bend from the cave.

Sascha leaned against the side of the mountain as his breath came in hoarse gasps, then he ran on. As he came close to the cave entrance, he saw Irinova, cowering down behind one of the boulders. Between them, facing him on the path, bloody, frothing and enraged, was the dragon.

It thrust its head at him and roared furiously. Sascha dodged to one side, frantically looking for something, a weapon, anything, then he spied a great rock wedged into the hillside at his feet. He crouched down and tried to pick it up but it held fast, slippery in the black mud; he could hear Irinova's muffled cries and the snorting of the dragon, and dug faster to free the rock. Pulling it loose at last, he took it in both hands, then as his muscles quivered and cramped, lifted it up over his head, took two paces toward the dragon, and hurled it with all his strength.

The next five seconds were an eternity.

The stone struck the dragon's shoulder as it raised up on its rear legs; thrown off balance, the beast wavered on the rock ledge. Irinova began to crawl, then run, past the dragon, toward Sascha, but as it toppled over the side, the very end of the dragon's tail tangled in Irinova's skirts, taking her with it.

The bellow of the dragon and Irinova's scream echoed through the forest and for one second the whole world was quiet.

"Oh, no, dear God, blessed Mother, no..." Sascha ran back to the rockslide and picked his way downhill again, shaking with cold and shock. He found the dragon laying among the sharp rocks in the ravine, its neck twisted and broken, wings ripped apart. Irinova was nowhere to be seen.

"Sascha..." He scarcely heard her voice as it came from behind him.

"Irinova! Where are you?" He whirled, searching, then he saw her, on a small rock ledge, skirts crumpled around her.

"Irinova --" her name came out in a grieved sob as Sascha knelt and touched her pale cheek. "Where are you hurt, is it your leg, your arm --"

"I...No, I do not think so, only my head, Sascha, it hurts so terribly."

"I am taking you back to the cave..." He began to lift

her but stopped when she cried out.

"No! Please, no, Sascha, my head..." She clung tightly to his hand. "Listen. Do you not hear them?"

Indeed he did: the men and dogs were closer yet.

"They will find the dragon...and then they will find me. These are my neighbors, Sascha, they will take me home safely." She took a breath and grimaced."What you must do... is to go back into the cave..."

"No! I will not leave you."

She squeezed his hand harder. "Listen to me! Who knows what may come about if they catch you! Stay in the cave until tomorrow...then pack what you will, Sascha, and go. Travel down the water road to a new life..."

"I cannot do that, Irinova, I have no money."

"Sascha," she whispered, drawing him closer, "look to your map. What you need is there."

"Irinova-"

"Hush! They are nearly here! Promise you will do as I say!"

Sascha sobbed as he caressed her hair and kissed first her cheek, then her lips.

"Irinova, my love..."

"Sascha Petrovich, you are my first love, my greatest friend." She pulled him close to her and kissed him."Now, you must go."

As he stood, he wiped tears from his eyes, leaving a muddy streak across his face, then Sascha turned and vanished into the forest.

"That wretch! How could he leave you, alone and

blind..."

"Drushka, Drushka, calm yourself! I made him go, for his sake. And I was not blind, not when he left me, indeed one of the last things remember was his sweet face bending over me and kissing me goodbye. Only minutes later, Father and the men had found the dragon and the dogs led them to me. Oh, the dogs bayed and scented toward the cave and I held my breath, but the men called them back and took me home..."

"That I remember-"

"...then the headaches came, also the fever..."

"Mama and her sister tended to you for so long, they would not even let me come in..."

"...and when it was all over, then I was blind."

"Dearest Irinova," Drushka sighed. "And so...what ever became of Sascha? Where did he go?"

Irinova smiled and nodded. "Ah-- he went down the river just as he planned."

"But how, he had no money!"

Irinova laughed, as one sharing a secret joke, and clasped her hands together under her chin.

"Remember I told him 'look to your map'..." She fairly wriggled with mischief.

"Yes-"

"I wrapped my garnet necklace around it, that day in the cave. I am sure it bought him a fine boat at the first city he came to..."

"Irinova! I always wondered what became of that necklace--"

"It was the best use of it, Drushka."

"But how do you know he ever --"

Irinova took a deep breath. "Three years later, at Easter, a messenger brought a parcel along with a note, addressed to me..."

"Go on!"

"Father read it to me. I will remember it always. It said: 'Irinova- All my children will learn your fairy tales. I think of you every day. I am well and I hope and pray you are the same. Faithfully, S.'"

"What did Father say?"

"He asked who 'S' was. I laughed and cried all at once- when I could speak, I told him it was 'Sonia,' a girlhood friend from the village.

"'She has done well in life, to send you such a splendid present,' Father said, and then he began to tell me of it. But I made him stop and simply put it in my hands, for I was learning how to perceive things by touching them."

"Then what did he give you?"

Irinova smiled as she stood and carefuly made her way to the bookshelf by the window. Her fingertips lightly felt along the top and rested upon a small silver egg; picking it up, she returned to her chair and handed it to Drushka.

"Oh, such a beautiful Easter gift, the tiny carved rabbits and flowers..."

"It has a hinge and clasp, see if you can find them." Irinova sat forward in her chair, smiling in anticipation.

"Where..." Drushka turned the egg around. "Ah! Here!"

"Open it."

Drushka lifted the top of the egg; her sharp breath of

amazement mingled with Irinova's delighted laugh, for inside the hollow silver egg, its wings poised ready for flight, rested a tiny golden dragon.

^^^

# **BEAUTIFUL ORIGIN**

The McCracken sisters cooked supper together in their roomy kitchen every night. They moved from icebox, to sideboard, to stove, to sink, alternating positions efficiently in a sort of culinary square-dance.

"Now, Lally, don't be cross," begged Virdene McCracken, as she pumped water into a pan and set it on the stove.

"I am not cross, Virdene," answered her older sister Eulalia, chopping turnips on the cutting board.

"You are so, you only call me Virdene when you're really serious. Or mad."

Eulalia began chopping another turnip. "I thought we agreed to discuss any new additions to the budget," she said firmly.

"Well, we're discussing it now, aren't we?" Virdene asked brightly, tilting her head to one side.

Eulalia scooped up the turnips and dumped them into the pan of boiling water. "You are the most exasperating person!" she fumed, putting her hands on her hips.

Sensing weakness, Virdene pounced. "Well, Sing Wah has such a hand in the garden, don't you remember I bought vegetables from his cart all last summer? Weren't they delicious? Well, Alice Burkett told me that Sing Wah is tending her garden this year, she's just around the corner,

123

you know, and so I arranged for him to do our gardening after he's finished Burkett's." She paused for breath, then plunged ahead. "Now, remember how hot it was last summer, we got so dirty, and when the ground got so dry it was hard to plant, and we always had to water, and I got sunburned just like a red Indian..."

"Virdene, you're giving me a headache," Eulalia sighed, as she turned pieces of chicken sizzling in a skillet.

"...Sing Wah only charges fifty cents a week, and he has all his own gardening tools, and we won't have to buy any vegetables, and..."

"All right, all right."

"What?"

"By all means, engage the services of Sing Wah."

"Oh! You're the dearest sister! I'll set the table for us, oh and Lally, will you make the gravy please, please- you know when I do it it's all lumps, and while you do that, I'll make us some lemonade..."

Eulalia found herself laughing, as she eventually always did, at her sister Deenie's impulsive antics and magpie chatter. She had secretly dreaded starting the garden this year, anyway; spring was either cold and muddy or too hot and dry. They could squeeze fifty cents a week into the budget for Sing Wah somehow. There were three months of school left; she would set aside extra money and, of course, Deenie was right: they wouldn't need to buy vegetables.

"I am *so* tired," Virdene said, as they finished dinner.

"No wonder, with all your running around at school. Deenie, the teacher isn't required to join in games during recess..."

"But it's so much fun, and I wanted to teach them to play badminton..."

"Last term it was field-hockey, and I spent all winter stitching your ripped-up hems."

"You're such a dear. Can we please sleep late tomorrow? 'Til seven?"

Quong Wah was awakened long before seven, by a rooster's crow somewhere in China Alley. Automatically he left his bed, started a fire and filled the kettle to make tea. While the water heated, he took a small bowlful of cold rice and slipped into a tiny storage room in the back of the laundry.

"Eight Precious!" Quong Wah called softly. He made a faint clicking noise as he lifted the lid from a great square wicker basket and set the bowl inside. "Here is your food now, little one." He stroked the small, dark head, and then, leaving the basket lid ajar, left the room.

Quong Wah was one of thousands of Chinese who had left the Middle Kingdom in 1850, intent on finding their fortune in the California gold fields. But the 'Golden Land' had proved rich only in obstacles: prejudice and greed had driven them from mining. Undaunted, they signed onto crews to complete the railroad and, while discrimination still followed them like a hungry dog, wages were regularly forthcoming. With the railroad finished, they fanned out across the Sacramento valley, taking jobs as cooks, gardeners, and like Quong Wah, laundrymen.

Settling in Freeman, a small town north of the

Sacramento river, Quong Wah and a handful of fellow 'sojourners' had turned a row of boxy, one-story wooden buildings into their own community. Some, despairing of returning to China, sent for wives and raised families. Quong Wah, on the other hand, was sent his younger brother from San Francisco. Sing Wah was a slow-witted youth, amiable but in need of constant prodding; Quong Wah suspected his uncle Lim Wah had given him Eight Precious as a bribe for fostering Sing Wah. Whatever the reason, the little creature was a delight, and Quong Wah treasured his time with her.

Passing by the bunk where his brother lay snoring, he nudged Sing Wah.

"Wake up, brother. I have made tea. Start the rice while I go pump water for the laundry."

"Unnhhhh..."

Taking this for a reply, Quong Wah went to the front laundry area, shouldered the buckets, and went to the pump. He returned a short time later to find a pot of burned rice and Sing Wah asleep in a chair by the stove. Furious, he took off one of his heavy canvas slippers and began smacking Sing Wah about the head.

"Disgrace to your ancestors! Lazy pig!" he shouted, literally hopping with rage, on the foot that still wore a shoe.

"What, what?" Sing Wah held his arms around his head, dodging his brother's attack.

"Cannot even cook rice! Stupid tortoise!"

Now awake, Sing Wah slid sideways from the chair to escape Quong Wah's blows.

"Ah hah!" shouted Quong Wah triumphantly. "Now you are up! Help with the laundry vats!"

"But I'm hungry..."

"Eat burned rice," Quong Wah snapped, and stomped off still holding his shoe in his hand. Sing Wah poured himself a cup of tea and munched on a mouthful of dry, charred rice. Shrugging, he shuffled off to build the fire in the laundry.

The McCracken sisters both taught at the nearby school. The younger children were Virdene's charges, while Eulalia instructed the older ones. It was a calling that seemed natural; their mother had instructed not only the girls and their brother Robbie, but several cousins and neighbor children as well. A bright outspoken Scotswoman with a penchant for learning and a talent for entertaining, she had attracted children like a magnet. "Playing school at the McCracken's" was the only education many of them ever received, and at that was better than most. To the McCracken girls, learning was fun, and teaching was the most fun of all.

Still, by the end of the week their energy was often flagging. Eulalia found herself looking forward to the arrival of Sing Wah, and her emancipation from gardening. The next Friday afternoon, she arrived home to find a slight, youngish Chinese man at the front gate.

"Missy McCracken, Sing Wah," he began, with several quick bows. "I garden now?"

"Yes, yes."

"Where garden?"

"Oh. Yes, just a moment." Eulalia deposited her armload of books and papers on the front steps. "This way, Mr. Wah."

"Sing Wah, Sing Wah," he insisted, smiling, with more quick bows.

"Very well, Sing Wah." She motioned for him to follow her around the north side of the house, and pointed to the large patch of ground beyond. Abandoned snap-bean poles leaned here and there, alongside a wizened, moldy pumpkin.

"Ah," he smiled, with more bows. "I bring shovel, I dig, thank you, Missy McCracken." Bowing while walking backward, he then returned to the front of the house.

"My goodness, with all that bowing he reminds me of a flicker pecking for grubs in the walnut tree," Eulalia said to herself.

Sing Wah came round the corner, cheerfully wheeling a small wooden cart laden with shovels, hoes, and rakes. After a few more bows, he set to work clearing away the poles and other garden debris, singing to himself in a thin, twangy voice.

Eulalia watched him for a moment, then retrieved her books from the front steps and went inside. Just then Virdene arrived home and went straight for the kitchen. "I'm going to make us a lemonade," she called out. Then she noticed Sing Wah in the garden.

"Oh, there he is." She picked a lemon out of the basket. "Heavens, Lally, what's that screechy noise?"

"It's the gardener, singing to himself."

"Perhaps that's why they call him 'Sing' Wah,"

Virdene giggled, cutting the lemon in half.

"Well, I don't care if he sings Stephen Foster, just as long as the gardening gets done."

And get done it did, shoveled and planted, watered and weeded. Spring brought a promise of growth to the garden plot; Virdene was smug in taking credit for hiring Sing Wah; Eulalia tolerated her sister's crowing, secretly thrilled with the arrangement; and Sing Wah's screechy serenades continued. Everyone was happy, including Quong Wah.

Relieved that his brother had found gainful work, he had to admit that although slow as an ox, Sing Wah did possess a knack for growing things. Most of all, he rejoiced that Sing Wah was not constantly underfoot, and that he had more time to commune with Eight Precious.

As she grew, she was allowed to leave her basket more and more, to scurry about the laundry and poke her pointed nose into everything, always making her happy squeaking sound. When he was folding laundry far into the night, she perched on his shoulder, holding fast with her fine claws and gazing in fascination at the light from the kerosene lamp. Quong Wah doted upon her.

The eventual cold rainy spell in April caught Eulalia by surprise. She preferred hanging clothes out to dry in the spring sunshine, and despaired at having to drape wrung-out laundry down in the basement. But Sing Wah's arrival on a drizzly Friday afternoon changed all that.

The McCracken sisters were sitting out on their front

porch, cozy beneath the wide overhanging roof, watching the rain.

"I just love it, don't you Lally?" asked Virdene, snuggling down into her coat. "Doesn't it smell good!"

Eulalia turned up her coat collar. "I hope you like the smell of wet clothes too, because we're going to have to hang them indoors..."

"Oh, don't be such a stump." Virdene wriggled on the wicker settee, rearranging her skirt .

"Stop squirming," Eulalia said, poking her sister. Both began giggling, jabbing at each other, and didn't notice the wooden cart until it halted in front of their house.

One Chinese man was pulling it, and another sat on the back amid neatly-wrapped bundles, swinging his feet. They both wore bamboo coolie hats.

"What on earth..." Virdene whispered. The man sitting on the back stood up as the one in front let go of the handles, and both came up the McCracken's front walk.

"It's Sing Wah, but who is that with him?" Eulalia whispered back as the pair stood before them. Sing Wah began bobbing up and down, chattering away.

"Missy McCracken, I come tell you, I no work today, it too much rain. Rain good for garden. But I no work. I come tell you..."

A sharp word from the other brought him up short.

"I am Quong Wah. My brother, Sing Wah." He bowed, more slowly and with a bit more purposeful demeanor. He gestured back at the cart.

"I have laundry. We deliver, so I bring brother to tell you he not garden today."

Eulalia stood up and found herself bowing back. "Yes, thank you, Quong Wah. Thank you, Sing Wah." She looked past them at the wooden cart, then clasped her hands together, smiling broadly.

"Excuse me, Quong Wah, you said you have a laundry?" she asked.

"Yes, yes."

"How soon can I have my laundry done?" Eulalia persisted. Behind her she heard Virdene gasp.

"Rain stop, I pick up tomorrow, finish Sunday," Quong Wah replied.

"Splendid. And I must tell you what a fine job Sing Wah does in the garden."

"Thank you, Missy McCracken. I be back soon." With a single dignified bow, Quong Wah turned, took his brother by the elbow, and together they returned to the cart. Sing Wah hopped on the back, Quong Wah took up the handles, and the pair trundled off down the street.

As Eulalia peered after them through the drizzle, Virdene could no longer contain herself.

"Have you lost you mind? Lally, surely you're not going to let that man handle your clothing!"

Eulalia rolled her eyes. "For goodness sakes, Deenie! You talk as though I'd be wearing them at the time! Quong Wah does laundry. That means that he washes and irons clothes, and that, simpleton, means no clothesline in the basement!"

Virdene began to sputter a reply, but Eulalia held up her hand. "It's settled."

There was a pause, then Virdene muttered stubbornly,

"Well, I'm washing my own underwear."

Just then there was a cracking flash of light followed by a boom of thunder. The two sisters squealed and hugged onto each other, then began laughing hysterically. Rain pelted down in gray sheets and gusted up onto the porch, as the McCracken sisters retreated inside.

By the time Quong Wah and Sing Wah delivered the remaining bundles and returned to China Alley, they were soaked to the skin. Quong Wah hustled his brother inside and stoked up the stove, making rice for dinner while Sing Wah changed into dry clothes. When the rice was ready, he opened the basket for Eight Precious and held his rice bowl while the little creature gobbled down each grain, making little satisfied trilling sounds. Later as he was putting her in for the night, she perched on the edge of the basket, humming and squeaking happily, then stretched her slim neck and spread her tiny wings, flapping them.

Quong Wah gasped in delight. "So young, already you are wanting to fly! Eight Precious, you are surely the most amazing dragon of all!"

"She grow, need bigger basket," Sing Wah said, looking up from his rice bowl.

"Yes! You are right, brother." Sing Wah beamed and continued eating. Quong Wah worked far into the night, as the thunder cracked and boomed outside, crafting a laundry basket into a larger home for the little black dragon he so loved.

It seemed to Eulalia that each summer, the school term

ended just in time. When it became impossible to contain an entire classroom of children for one more day, when there were puppies and kittens in every barn, when the days were hot and long, with creeks for swimming and trees for climbing, mercifully, school was out. Not without joy, the McCracken sisters packed up classroom supplies and looked forward to time for themselves, to read, visit friends, or indulge in the slothful pastime of doing absolutely nothing.

Summer came to China Alley also. Evenings after the day's work, Chinese gathered outside, escaping their cramped living quarters. The sojourners talked, cooked on small charcoal braziers, ate, smoked, sang, and engaged in games of chance well into the night. Quong Wah joined them from time to time, but always returned to the laundry early, to be with Eight Precious. Just outside the back door of the laundry, in a setback space, a crape myrtle tree grew. Quong Wah permitted Eight Precious to stretch her wings there, gently tethered by a silken cord, while he fed her bits of rice, meat, and fresh fruit. As the nights became warmer, he would allow her to fly loose and circle the alley, enticing her back with a warbling whistle and a reward of sweet honey-cake.

Sing Wah was a hesitant spectator to Eight Precious. Never particularly fond of cats or dogs, he was positively leery of dragons. Their small claws, twining tails and flapping wings unnerved him, and he put his fingers in his ears to block out their warbles and screeches. As long as Eight Precious was on her silken leash, Sing Wah felt safe from dragon-attacks, and Quong Wah was reassured that his beloved pet would not fly away.

It was one of many hot July evenings. The McCracken sisters sat out on the screened-in porch at the rear of their house, sipping lemonade. Each held a cardboard fan and attempted to cool off by waving it sporadically. Eulalia at last put her glass down with a thump on the small table between them.

"Well, I'm not waiting for the breeze to come, I'm going to be comfortable." She reached down, unbuttoned her shoes, kicked them off and tugged off her stockings. "Ahhh," she sighed, leaning back in her chair and wriggling her bare feet. Virdene watched her, wide-eyed and impish, then followed suit.

"D'you suppose this is quite ladylike?" she asked, stuffing her stockings into her shoes.

"Deenie, I am on my own porch of my own home..."

"...our home," Virdene corrected, poking her.

"...exactly, and I intend to be comfortable. Besides, Mama would've done the same thing."

"And Daddy tickled her feet, remember? And she laughed so hard Robbie started to cry..."

Eulalia smiled at the memory. The McCracken 'Highland sense of humor' had made for a lively childhood. As dusk turned the sky to a rich cobalt blue, she gazed out at the yard, then impulsively got up and stood by the screen. She squinted, scarcely able to make them out, black-on-blue, tiny forms swooping and gliding about the treetops.

"What is it, Lally?" Virdene asked, leaning forward.

Eulalia stood rooted with fascination. "Bats," she answered. "They're so magical, Deenie!"

"Eww!" Virdene scrunched back into her chair, one hand automatically up to her hair. "They can't get in here, can they?"

"Not with the door shut, silly goose," Eulalia snorted, still watching.

"Don't they bite, and get caught in your hair?"

"Virdene, they eat mosquitoes, for goodness' sake! And I suppose if you were fool enough to go out without a hat, you might snag one." Eulalia laughed as her sister squirmed and made faces. Then she picked up the empty glasses. "I'm getting us some more lemonade." Opening the back door, she added, "Stay inside, now."

"Lal-*lee*!" Virdene heard her sister laughing all the way into the kitchen. "Wear a hat indeed," she muttered to herself, then her curiosity got the best of her and she tiptoed to the screen, craning her neck upward. "As long as they can't get in..." she whispered. Did they make noises, she wondered, shifting from one foot to the other as she tried to make out where they were. Virdene almost had her nose pressed to the screen when with a warbling chirp, something streaked right past her face, something black, with  flapping wings and a long tail straight out behind.

"Yeeeek!" She jumped back in fright, tripped over her shoes, and sprawled on her backside, striking her head on the table. "Lally! Help! Eeek!"

"Good God in heaven, Virdene, what is it?" Eulalia came from the kitchen on a dead run, holding up her skirt in both hands. Seeing her sister flat on her back on the porch, she knelt down and took hold of her hand.

"What's wrong, Deenie? Is...is someone out there?" Eulalia turned toward the screen, and grabbed a shoe to throw at any potential intruder.

"No, it's...it's...It was a bat, Lally, a great big bat the size of a possum!"

"A bat that big?"

"Yes, and it flew right past me, and it had a tail too!"

Relieved somewhat, Eulalia put the shoe down and helped Virdene to her feet. "Are you all right?"

"Yes...ow...no. I hit my head on the table..."

Eulalia hugged her sister and patted her back. "Poor Deenie, attacked by a bat." Then she began to giggle in spite of herself.

"'tisn't funny," Virdene began, then she too started to laugh. "But I swear, Lally, on the Bible, that creature was this long!" She held her hands two feet apart.

"H'mm. Well...imagine the size of the mosquitoes it must eat," Eulalia mused.

"That does it." Virdene picked up her shoes and socks and marched to the door. "Hot and stuffy or not, I'm going in the house where it's safe."

Eulalia collected her own shoes as she chuckled to herself. How Deenie did carry on sometimes, she thought. It was only a bat.

In China Alley, Quong Wah also saw the sky become darker, and when Eight Precious went up for her evening flight, she suddenly disappeared over the rooftops. He waited a few moments, then began calling her. As long minutes passed, worry began to gnaw on Quong Wah like a rat. What mischief might the little dragon get into? Surely no harm would come to her? His neck began to ache as he stood, head back, eyes riveted on the sky above. Every time she flew free, Eight Precious always returned to him; where could she possibly be? Sing Wah even came from inside, wondering why his brother was taking so long. Quong Wah kept up his whistling call, and finally, though he could not see her at first, heard her answering him. His heart pounded with joy as she dropped down and landed gracefully upon his outstretched wrist, her tail wrapping around his arm.

"Aiiieee!" Sing Wah stepped back in alarm at the dragon's quick movements, but seeing his brother's relief, nodded and smiled. Quong Wah scolded Eight Precious for worrying him so, then promised her treats for her obedience as he carried her inside. Sing Wah followed, and the back door to the laundry closed without a sound.

Eulalia rationalized that, although the dry summer heat could be nearly unbearable, it made for a cornucopia of produce from the garden, and never so much so as this year. By August she and Virdene had run out of canning jars once and needed an emergency order from Spiller's General Store. Beans, peas, carrots, pickles- the basement shelves were groaning. They had more than enough. One morning when Sing Wah was tending to the garden in his usual slow-moving fashion, she approached with a proposition.

"We really can't eat all this food, Sing Wah. If you like, you may take what is left and sell it from your vegetable cart."

"Sing Wah sell, for you?"

"You may keep half of whatever money you make, for your hard work. "

"Keep half money from sell?"

"Yes, Sing Wah. Surely you have something you, um, save your money for?"

He nodded, smiling. "I save, I save for Beautiful Origin." He kept on smiling and nodding as he raked.

"Well then, that's settled. Be sure and get yourself a drink of water from the pump before you go, Sing Wah."

"Yes, Missy McCracken."

Later, over lunch, Eulalia told Virdene of the arrangement.

"I think that's very kind. Now, please, do we have to can anything this week?"

Eulalia laughed. "No, but we're going to dry apricots from the Porter's tree."

Virdene sighed with relief. "I wonder what the 'Beautiful Origin' means?"

"I think it's another name for China. They must miss their country terribly."

"'The land of Beautiful Origin'...oh, Lally, that's so sweet and sad, it's almost poetic."

"Speaking of poetry, we have books due at the library. Help me clear away here and we'll go." Virdene daydreamed as she stacked dishes, murmuring 'Beautiful Origin' and dawdling so that Eulalia had to give her a pinch to get her going.

Sing Wah gleaned the last of the produce from the McCracken's garden and brought Eulalia a handful of coins after market day, half of which she returned to him as agreed. Sing Wah was happy with his money, Eulalia was happy the food had not been wasted, and Virdene was most happy that canning season was over. Still, both sisters missed the gardener's quirky geniality.

"Quong Wah was here not five minutes ago, delivering the laundry," Virdene called from the kitchen. It was a Saturday morning, and Eulalia had gone out returning library books.

"Tarnation!" exclaimed Eulalia in disappointment. "I missed him! I meant to ask about Sing Wah..."

"I imagine he helps his brother with the laundry," Virdene began.

"Yes, well, I imagine you can help me hang ours up and put it away."

Across town, it was well into afternoon when Quong Wah finished up the last of his deliveries. He trundled the empty cart around through the alley and opened the back door.

"Sing Wah?" he called out, but heard no answer. He checked the front of the shop, found it empty, and returned to their living quarters. Quong Wah pulled aside the heavy curtain that partitioned off their beds, and gasped.

There was a sickly sweet, musky smell in the air, and on his bunk, Sing Wah lay unmoving, glassy eyes half-closed, holding an opium pipe loosely in one hand.

Inundated by disappointment, anger, worry and

shame, Quong Wah numbly let the curtain fall. Then he sought out the one being that would restore his peace of mind: Eight Precious. Gently he took her from her cage, and walked with her to the darkened, deserted laundry room. There he sat on a soap box, rocking back and forth, stroking the tiny dragon's head.

"I know...Uncle warned me...brother Sing Wah is tempted by vices...I thought by keeping him occupied, he would be too busy for trouble." Quong Wah drew a shaky sigh. "Sing Wah has no money...how has he paid for opium? All laundry money is in the bank." Eight Precious turned round on his knee and stared up at him, then rubbed her face against his chin. Quong Wah leaned forward, cradling her, and began moaning softly.

"I fear the worst...Sing Wah has stolen money from his employers...those kind enough to let him work in their gardens...he has betrayed their trust...and brought dishonor to our family." The room grew dark as Quong Wah sat with his little dragon, drawing consolation from her. It was early evening when he rose and made his way back to the kitchen.

Quong Wah lit the kerosene lamp and composed a long letter to Uncle Lim Wah. As he wrote, Eight Precious sat on the edge of her basket, trilling, then flew to his shoulder, where she gazed at the light and occasionally nibbled at Quong Wah's pen. She leaned her head against his jaw and a tear slid down his lined cheek, falling upon the paper.

The next morning, Quong Wah arose and walked to the post office to mail his letter. Back at the laundry, he made tea, fetched water for the vats, and made rice. Only then did he shake Sing Wah awake.

"Here is tea, brother. Hot and strong. Wake up."

Foggily, Sing Wah took the teacup, becoming more awake with each sip.

"Uncle will be coming soon," Quong Wah began, as he filled two bowls with rice. "He will be taking you back to San Francisco with him." Sing Wah nodded cheerfully, scooping rice into his mouth, while Quong Wah sat quietly in a corner and shared his breakfast with Eight Precious.

Two days later, both brothers met Uncle Lim at the afternoon train. That night after dinner when Sing Wah was asleep, Quong Wah at last unburdened himself.

"I apologize ten thousand times, Uncle. I have failed..."

"You have not failed, Quong Wah. Sing Wah is your brother, yes—but he is not your son. We all understand the trials you have endured. No, Quong Wah, you have decided correctly. You are not a failure."

Quong Wah managed to hold back tears of relief.

"There is one indulgence I beg of you."

"I will do what I can, Nephew."

"Please...take Eight Precious with you."

Uncle Lim gasped. "You no longer want her?"

Quong Wah could remain composed no longer. Tears fell as he took one of his uncle's hands.

"She has been my complete joy, I treasure her beyond understanding."

"Then why-"

Quong Wah drew a deep, shaking breath before

continuing. "She deserves to fly free, over the mountains and rivers of China, the land of her birth. Here she has none of her own kind. She is isolated, as are we."

At this, Uncle Lim nodded in solemn agreement.

"Uncle, if you do no other thing for me in my miserable life, promise me you will send her on the next ship, and return her to the Middle Kingdom, to live out her days in safety and happiness."

Uncle Lim then grasped both of Quong Wah's hands tightly.

"I promise, Quong Wah, and I honor your complete and unfailing wisdom." The two wept quietly on a cool autumn evening in China Alley. The next day, two Chinese men, one younger, and one older carrying a large bamboo basket, boarded the train for San Francisco.

Virdene speculated that Sing Wah was indeed gone, not having seen him for some time. Eulalia preferred getting right to the heart of the matter, and when Quong Wah next delivered laundry, she inquired about his brother.

"Has Sing Wah returned to China?" she asked, taking the brown paper bundle from him.

Quong Wah paused, expressionless, then nodded. "Yes."

"Back to 'Beautiful Origin'," Virdene added, dreamily.

Quong Wah turned, startled, and stared at Virdene. "You know 'Beautiful Origin'?" he asked urgently.

"Well, no, I mean, he said..." Virdene stammered, taken aback.

"The garden grew more than we needed," Eulalia

explained, intervening. "I told Sing Wah he could pick the rest, sell it at the farmers' market, and keep half of the money for himself..."

"Sing Wah have money?" Quong Wah asked in disbelief.

"...and he said he was saving for 'Beautiful Origin'," Virdene added.

"Sing Wah have money," Quong Wah repeated. Then, with a dazed expression, he turned, walked down the steps, and continued pushing his cart down the street.

The McCracken sisters exchanged puzzled looks, then Eulalia noticed she still had money in her hand.

"Quong Wah!" she called after him, but he was too far away. "I forgot to pay him, Deenie."

"I'll take it to him tomorrow. I really believe he's lonely."

After breakfast the following day, Virdene walked downtown on several small errands, including a stop at the laundry. Back at home, she dutifully reported all the local gossip as she put the kettle on for tea.

"Lally, Quong Wah misses his brother terribly."

"I'm sure he does, just the way I would miss you..."

"Oh, Lally, you're a dear, hand me the sugar bowl, please."

Eulalia wrinkled her nose at her sister. "What did Quong Wah say..."

"Well, when I went in, he didn't see me at first, he was back by those great enormous washing tubs, talking to himself, in Chinese..."

"Then how could you understand him?"

"Because I heard Sing Wah's name, and then he said something was 'precious.' It made me sad to see him, Lally, do you know, he was so upset, he was crying."

~~~

Developers in Freeman, excavating the site of the old China Alley one hundred years later, unearthed many interesting artifacts. Among these were ivory chopsticks, soup bowls, tea cups, cooking pots, and scores of square metal tins with tight-fitting lids. These were covered with Chinese calligraphy, and were determined by oriental antiquities experts to be opium tins. The writing, when translated, appeared to be brand names for the opiate, such as 'Eye of Peacock' and 'Purple Lotus.' But the most numerous tins, therefore arguably the most popular, were the variety called 'Beautiful Origin.'

∧∧∧

# THE PLACE BETWEEN

Back then, so many years ago, the world was simpler. Superstitions and folk tales were intermingled with religious practices and everyday customs, unlike the present time when they are easily dismissed as only harmless children's diversions. That is why I kept this to myself for so long: the knowledge that, had I revealed everything, no one would have believed me. Now I do not bother with what others think; I alone know the story is true.

I helped close up at the milliner's shop where I worked, and hurried to the druggist's for some headache powder. As Mr. Burnham, the chemist, took my order, I heard from the back the cheery drone of a concertina and someone singing a strange, foreign song. The music seemed to come closer, and suddenly from around the corner of the office a face appeared, blue eyes and black curly hair under a tweed cap, and a smile so mischievous I laughed on the spot.

"Have you by chance seen any fairies?" he asked, whereupon I laughed again, shaking my head. "They'll be coming out soon now, for it's neither work nor play time, but between..."

The chemist handed me my packet. As he passed by,

he pushed the young man's cap down over his forehead, chuckling. "Go on now, Kevan, none of your Irish stories for this lady." He yanked a thumb at Kevan. "Him and the fairies..."

The young man grinned, pulling his cap back up.

"I can see you're of no help closing up," Mr. Burnham clucked. "Be a good lad and walk Miss Harrold home, then."

"Yes, sir." Kevan laid aside the concertina with a wheezing thump, and held the door open for me.

I headed down the street, with Kevan striding along, from time to time jigging round a lamp-post, humming to himself.

"Are you really Irish?" I asked.

"As Paddy's pig," he laughed. "Kevan Keane, at your service." We came to a corner. "Which way, Miss Harrold?" he asked, standing smartly at attention.

I waved a hand to the right. "It's Leticia, and my flat's right here, the second door."

He took off his cap. "When might I see you again?"

"Well...if I have another headache...."

"Then I wish you headaches, sore feet, the ague..."

"Oh, and a fine chemist you are, to be sure?" I chided back.

He leaned against the post by the steps. "Not at all; really I just live above the shop and give Burnie a hand when I can. I clerk at the woolbrokers in Chesterfield Street." For a moment his face became serious and I noticed how handsome he really was. "I want a real future, Leticia; property, position..." then he laughed again and straightened his cap. "And a date with you to go to the pub tomorrow night."

And go we did. In the weeks that followed, we played darts at the pub, fed ducks in the park, had tea at my flat, took long walks. And whenever we were out together, Kevan would begin yet another tale. He saw things through eyes of his Celtic ancestors and believed in lore I could not begin to share; when he spoke of the old ways of generations long back, his eyes would glow wide in wonder and his voice would come like music, with a lilt and sway to each word. Yet in all the tales he told, never did I learn the signs of danger, so warnings I might have seen were unknown to me.

Over fish and chips at my flat one evening, Kevan noticed I was unusually quiet, and I confessed to being concerned over the war.

He cocked his head to one side. "Ah, Leticia, you worry so. If there's one thing you should have a care about..." he raised one eyebrow at me.

"And what is that?"

"...my stealing the last piece of fish!" And with that he snatched it from the oily newspaper. I tried to grab it and he demanded a kiss for ransom which I playfully gave; but to no avail for he gobbled down every bit. As consolation, he spun yet another story, this time of a legendary Irish slayer of dragons. I began to clean up, and he insisted in taking the rubbish out to the incinerator.

I could hear him singing again, but this time it seemed more like a chant, and he clapped his hands several times.

I tiptoed outside then. It was not day, not quite night time, and twilight shadows obscured the back garden. As I approached Kevan I touched his arm and he gave a jump, startled.

"Another song about an Irish hero?" I asked.

"No, no, Letty, just...some of the old ways. Come inside now, before we catch a chill." I took his arm, but only to hold his hand, for it wasn't in the least bit cold.

We had just come inside when I thought I heard it: I waited, then it came again, a short, firm knock at the front door. "Yes, who is it?" I called as I walked into the hall, but there was no reply. Upon opening the door, I saw her for the first time.

She was not as tall as I, yet she stood back away from the door so that her gaze seemed level with mine. Her eyes were glass-green, and her skin had the finish of a china peach. Hair the color of brandy framed her face and hung thick and wavy around her shoulders.

"Yes?" I began.

Those green eyes looked past me; no, *through* me. "Kevan."

I turned, and found him standing right behind me.

"You don't remember me?" Her voice was clear, with a trace of accent.

"I..." Kevan frowned a bit, shaking his head slowly.

"Years. Years have passed since I last saw anyone...in the family."

Kevan's hand pushed at his chin. "My cousins? They-"

"Yes." She held out her hand and he took it. Awkwardly I stood aside and for a full minute took in the two of them, Kevan holding her delicate fingertips and she regarding him with an unwavering gaze.

"Ah...won't you please come in?" I said.

As if brought out of a trance, Kevan started and let go her hand. "Leticia, this is my cousin..." he halted.

"Eridwyn," she finished for him.

"May I take your coat?" I offered, as the three of us entered the parlor. She seemed not to have heard, and then I noticed she wore, instead of a coat, a cloak of black brocade. From beneath its folds she pulled a roll of parchment papers which she handed to Kevan.

"These I bring, for you."

He took the bundle and started to undo it. One graceful hand stopped him. "I must be on my way."

"Oh, but..." He held out a hand to her and she touched it lightly as she passed. I wasn't used to seeing Kevan befuddled.

"We'll meet again...dear cousin." She laughed softly. "I'm certain of it." Then as her cape swished softly behind her, she glided to the door and saw herself out.

I stood by the sideboard, amazed by the entire incident. Kevan slid a tie of wrinkled ribbon from the roll of parchment and straightened the pages. As he scanned them, one after the other, I watched his face go from curiosity to surprise to glee.

"Leticia!" He brandished the sheaf of paper in the air excitedly. "This...it's the most wonderful news!" He put his hands on my shoulders and kissed me on both cheeks.

"Tell me, tell me!" I demanded.

"...an old will, apparently lost for some time, it says

here I've ten thousand pounds in the bank..."

"Kevan!"

"...and this, this..." he shuffled through the pages and pulled one free. "A house, Letty. I've a house, in the country." The gravity of it all seemed to strike him at once, for he sat down heavily in the chair by the hearth and simply stared at me, nonplussed.

"Your cousin," I blurted out. "We must thank her for seeking you out..." I ran to the door, opened it and peered out into the graying twilight, up the street and down, but no one was about, no one wearing a long black cloak. Then, unlike earlier, I did feel a chill.

The weekend that followed, Kevan moved into his house. It was a charming cottage, set back from a lane alternately shaded with oaks and dotted with open fields. He hired a van, although it was scarcely needed to haul Kevan's scant possessions from the room at the chemist's shop. I rode with the driver, a likeable old fellow, and Kevan sat in the back happily playing his concertina and shouting out songs the whole way.

"Oh...here we are, this is it," I said suddenly, and the van jerked to a halt.

"Now that's one on me," the driver said amiably. "Here I've been driving this road these years and never once noticed this house before today." As he pushed back his cap, he walked to the rear of the van where Kevan was already unloading boxes. Good-naturedly he brushed off our protests, helped us unload, and insisted on seeing the house and the back garden as well. He lived in the nearby village and told us the names of the baker, grocer and butcher.

"Has a bit of a heavy thumb on the scale, so mind when he weighs up your beef," he warned me with a wink. "A right proper tangle this is," he commented, surveying the garden. Indeed it was, with its granite bench barely visible under vines and branches. "And say now." He stopped and leaned a strong hand on the weathered fence. The post was worn and the rails had fallen away, leaving a gap where it came together in a corner. "This will want fixing." He gave Kevan a serious look, then tipped his cap. "I'll be off now."

Kevan saw the driver to his van and paid him. By the time he walked back, I had cleared a space on the garden bench. "I'm having a rest," I announced, and sat. "What did he mean, the fence 'would want fixing'?"

"Ah, it's a place between, neither fence nor open," Kevan said bending down. "A faerie place," he added.

I was about to ask what that had to do with repairs, when I noticed a silver chain, just inside his open shirt collar.

"Hello, what's this?" I put my hand on the back of his neck.

"Oh." His hand went to his shirt front, almost in a nervous fashion. "It's a good-luck charm, of sorts."

"Let me see," I persisted.

He pulled at the chain and held up, between thumb and forefinger, a boxy cross, no bigger than a postage stamp, covered with an intertwined design.

"It's nothing fancy," Kevan said abruptly, dropping the chain back into his shirt. He leaned on the broken fence, gone all quiet and thoughtful.

Altogether with the issue of the broken fence, this exchange gave me rather an excluded feeling, that something was being kept from me. Very much like the gap in the wood fence, I felt things were not connecting where they should. I have wondered many times if, had I spoken up, events would have unfolded differently.

Although we didn't speak of it, the war in Europe drew still closer, however our jobs kept us both busy and we occupied our thoughts with furnishing the house and clearing up the garden. One overcast Saturday afternoon we labored, cutting back and trimming until tired and sore. A fine mist began which promised to turn into rain.

"I'm for packing in in," I admitted, stowing my gloves and shears in the tiny potting shed.

"Ah, where's my hearty country lass?" Kevan teased, scraping the mud from his boots.

"Well sir, that I do not know, but the milliner's clerk is going inside to make your tea," I laughed, and ducked into the kitchen door.

He remained out a bit longer, and from the kitchen I heard him clapping his hands and chanting another old song. Then the rain began properly, and he was at the door.

"Chamomile tea is ready, honey's in the pot, and bread and jam on the table."

"No biscuits?"

"If it's biscuits you want, then you must tell me a story," I bargained.

He tilted his head thoughtfully, then lit a lamp and

drew me to a chair. He pulled me down onto his lap and began a saga of Celtic warriors and their queens, brutal and brave, aided by magic and spurred on by strength. I leaned my head upon his shoulder, listening to his voice and the rain falling outside. He stroked my hair as he talked, them slowly drew me close and kissed me.

A sound outside made us both jump. I began to giggle, embarrassed, and scrambled up for a look out at the back garden.

"It's Eridwyn." Her cloak swayed behind her as she proceeded in her fluid fashion to the front door. I went ahead to open it for her and called out as she approached.

"It's slippery. Grab hold of the wrought-iron railing."

She froze at my words, took one look at the bannister alongside the brick steps, and deliberately backed up. Then she turned and went the length of the path, back to the kitchen door. I watched her, thinking Kevan's cousin an odd bit of business to say the least.

Kevan had let her in, and I returned just in time to hear her say,

"It's so wet out, I didn't want to muck up your front entry, so I came straight to the kitchen."

"Of course," he agreed. "Let me take your cloak."

I lit another lamp, then took her wrap to hang it up. I could see it was actually the darkest green, with a tiny pattern of interlacing strands and knots overall. The clasp was actually two silver dragon's-heads, holding in their teeth the chain that bound the cloak together.

"We were having tea," I offered, returning to the kitchen. "Would you like..." As before, she ignored me, eyes only for Kevan. Her long fingers brushed hair from her face as she spoke to him.

"Dear cousin, I came by to see if you were settled into your fine house."

"Indeed, it's been home since the first day," Kevan said enthusiastically. "It's grand. We tried to find you so we could thank you, but..."

"It is rightfully yours, as is all you claim." Eridwyn sat straight in a chair next to Kevan, her eyes enormous in the lamp light. "Are you truly happy here, cousin? For there are finer places in the world..."

Kevan got up and went to the window. "Oh yes, truly happy. Yet...for how much longer, who can say. Every day the war is closer, more imminent..." I looked at him surprised, for he had not voiced this concern with me, then realized he had been sparing me worry. I know I blushed, as I felt my love for him fill my heart.

Eridwyn lowered her head, then looked up at him underneath thick lashes. "Do you fear to fight, then?"

I sat up straight, a retort at the ready, but Kevan answered back.

"Go I will, and fight I will, I'm not afraid." With one hand he gripped the back of a chair, gesturing with the other. "It's the not knowing where one's going to be, or when...I'd as soon sign up and have it over."

Her green eyes fixed on him, she nodded after a moment. Cat-like, she rose to her feet. "Now I really must go. I've a cab waiting."

I fetched her cloak from the rack in the front room and felt how light-weight it was for such ornate fabric: light and...something more...

Kevan took the cloak from me and fastened in round Eridwyn's shoulders. She opened the door and stepped out into the rain.

"Until...next time, cousin?" she said huskily to Kevan, then the front door closed behind her.

Next morning we went out for a walk and stopped by the front gate to admire a rainbow across the field. While there, I gave a good long look at the road and remembered. Eridwyn had claimed she hired a cab; yet the surface of the road was unbroken and firm, with no tire tracks, the entire length of the property. It made me shiver.

Back inside, the cold feeling stayed despite morning tea. I wrapped a comforter around me like a cloak. Then I recalled from the night before..

Eridwyn's cloak, with its biting-dragons clasp, which she wore upon arriving in the pouring rain, walking back and forth outside. When I took it from Kevan to hang up, holding it in my hands... it had been completely dry.

It was a week later when I was puttering around in the garden and a 'Hallo!' from the road brought me to the front gate. It was our friend the van driver, halted in the road.

"Just thought I'd stop by and see how you was getting on," he said cheerfully. "By the way, did your young man fix the back fence?"

"Well, no, I don't think so." Kevan hadn't seemed to think it that urgent, and truthfully I hadn't noticed.

The old man nodded slowly, then climbed briskly into

the van and started the engine. "Take care, miss," he said in parting, his tone serious. Then he waved and chugged off down the lane.

It was that odd time of day, neither afternoon nor evening. The light from the window was poor when I settled down to read, yet when I lit the lamp it scarcely made a difference. It was of no consequence, for as I picked up my book once more, Kevan charged into the room, seized my hands and began to dance us round the room.

He was chattering away like a monkey, and it was some minutes before I could understand what he was saying. From his coat pocket, he produced an envelope bearing a military insignia.

"I've a rank! I'm a yeoman, attached to the Head Office in London!" I shook my head, still confused. "That means I'll stay right here, in all probability throughout the war!" He waltzed me round the room again at a dizzying rate, then dropped suddenly to one knee, taking my hand in his.

"Marry me, Leticia, then I'll be the happiest man on earth!"

I squeezed his hand in both of mine. "Kevan, my darling, why didn't you ask sooner?"

He sprang to his feet, waving his hands around him. "I wanted us to be properly set, have a home of our own, to offer you security, and more than just fish and chips in a rented flat!"

"Oh, you silly goose! My only answer is yes, yes!" My arms around him, I held him tightly. That instant we were so happy.

Impulsively he clapped his hands, declaring we should have a celebration and offering to pour sherry. In the kitchen he rummaged in a drawer and called out that he couldn't find the corkscrew. I got up to light another lamp just as he entered from the kitchen. There was a noise from the corner, and we both turned. I gasped to see Eridwyn standing in the shadows.

Her black eyes blazed with hatred, and her hair bristled about her. Long fingers left eerie images on the wall behind her as she folded back the front of her cape.

"You, Kevan Keane, are most unwise." As always her words were only for him. "You have accepted my help, indeed summoning me at your convenience. And now, I find that you prefer the affections of another."

Kevan stood in the doorway, his face wary and impassive. He looked like a stranger.

"These spells I have made for you: The Making of Wealth, The Shielding from War. Is that not so?"

Spells, what spells, I wanted to shout, but I stood numb and silent instead, watching as Kevan nodded slowly.

"You knew the old ways sufficiently to call me forth. I have done as you bid, and now you think you can spurn me?" She laughed, this time an ugly, shrill sound. "You shall repay me, Kevan. I will have pleasure, if not with you, then by savoring your fate."

Kevan regarded her with bold confidence. Still he said nothing, only his hand slowly went to his throat; I saw his fingers reach for the necklace, then grope frantically. He went pale as an awful look of recognition and horror crossed his face.

"Oh, please..." I began, placing my hand on her arm. That one instance she did look in my direction, with such venom in her gaze I stood frozen. To this day, my cheek stings when I recall the slap of her hand, quick as a whip.

"Leave her unharmed!" Kevan cried out.

"Oh, as always, I shall do your bidding, my *love*." Her words were hateful and bitter. "I shall leave you both now. Kevan - you know what you must do to summon me."

Then she flung both her arms wide. There was a loud roar, and the lamps seemed to explode, plunging the room into darkness. I think that I screamed. An icy wind swept through the room, taking my breath away; I heard her terrible laugh echo in the hall, the slam of doors, then silence.

I trod on broken glass, reaching the sideboard at last. I felt about for another lamp but found only candles; matches burned my trembling fingertips as I managed to light one. I heard Kevan's voice, a desperate whisper somehow changing into a groan, calling my name for what was to be the last time.

In the dull candlelight I saw what she had done. I made to scream, but clapped both hands over my mouth. I bit my fingers and held my breath, heart pounding, until I was close to fainting.

Across the room from me, a blue-purple-hued dragon huddled, cringing and confused, gazing at me with mournful blue eyes. If never before had I helped him, I knew I must help him then, if I loved him at all. And so I sank to the floor and began to talk soothingly.

"Kevan?"

The dragon nodded, its scales glittering in the candlelight. I bit my thumb until I tasted blood. "What she said...it was so? You had these things conjured for you?" Again it nodded.

"Did you not know she wanted you for herself?" It sat still, quivering, then shook its head.

Then I reasoned what had happened. As a minion of the Faerie world, Eridwyn had granted Kevan's foolish wishes and hoped in the bargain to have him for her own. But when spurned, her icy revenge had exacted a terrible toll: she had returned to her land, the place between, and left us together, but satisfied that never again would Kevan kiss my lips or hold me in his arms. No charm was powerful enough to spare him.

"Can we not call her to return, perhaps she will change her mind..." It shook its beautiful head slowly, scales luminous in the candlelight.

"You summoned her at other times, did you not - she said that you knew how..." The dragon nodded miserably.

I paced about, stepping over broken glass, then quickly seized pen and paper from the writing desk.

"You will tell me." I rested myself on a footstool opposite the dragon, which was the size of a mastiff. "I will recite the alphabet, and you are to nod your head at the letter you wish me to write. You will spell out letter by letter what you must do."

I began. "A?...B?...C?" The dragon nodded, its jetblack whiskers quivering. The message crawled across the paper, and at length we were finished.

# TEN DRAGON TAILS

The dragon shrieked, its tortured cry that of a beast trapped in the forest. Ebony claws dug into the carpet in despair and grief as I read aloud the words:

'C-L-A-P  M-Y  H-A-N-D-S'

∧∧∧

# <u>NESSIE</u>

In the warm mid-afternoon sun, a light breeze pulled clouds along like lazy kites. An ancient automobile slowed and pulled off onto a clearing bordered on two sides with gorse bushes and thistle. The clearing gave way to a rocky outcropping, steep but accessible to the sure-footed, that provided access down to the loch .

"Will we see her today d'ye think, Granpa?"

"I dinna ken, lad. You canna whistle her up like a sheepdog, now."

Andrew Mackenzie put his pipe in his pocket and opened the creaky door of the auto, looking up just in time to see his grandson Jamie, binoculars in hand, halfway across the clearing.

Their son Rob, his wife Corlyn, and son Jamie had spent holidays with Andrew and Florrie since Jamie was a wee baby. When Corlyn died of tuberculosis, Rob had sent him for entire summers; then World War II broke out. While Rob Mackenzie did not consider Scotland as a prime target for German bombing raids, to be on the safe side he sent Jamie to live near Inverness with his grandparents, reasoning that German U-boats in Loch Ness were even less likely than an attack on Edinburgh by the Luftwaffe.

After school each day, armed with sticks and rocks, Jamie and his young cohorts had diligently combed the streets and alleys looking for Nazi paratroopers. Eager to do their part for war effort, they surveyed the horizon for hours on end with spyglasses and binoculars. While the longed-for end of war brought relief, it left an entire county of young boys with no mission in life. Thus, with school out, Jamie eagerly accompanied his grandfather Mackie on various errands. One such expedition in early summer took them past Loch Ness.

"Yonder Urquardt Castle," Mackie gestured across the loch. "Keep a sharp eye, you may see the Loch Ness monster," he chuckled, unprepared for what was to come.

"Oh?"

"Aye, near here's where what they call the Loch Ness monster was first sighted, it's been, ah, ten years now..."

"A real sea monster?

"Well, sort of a sea-monster, like..."

"Here? Right here? Stop, granpa, stop!"

Life for Mackie had certainly not been the same. Jamie was determined to return at every opportunity that presented itself; binoculars trained on the expanse of water, he was once more on the lookout, not for Nazis, but Nessie.

Perched on a squarish granite boulder, Jamie was soon scanning the shore opposite them, with its rocky hillside and small pebbled beach.

Mackie got out his pipe and book.

"Over there, across the lake- D'ye ever fish there?" Jamie asked, lowering the binoculars.

"Aye, a time back. But two years now, I've got not a thing but a sore arse from sittin' on them rocks."

Jamie laughed and resumed watch.

"Still on the lookout for Jerries?"

"Don't know...y'got to be alert, though, the newspaper says there might be fudge- fudge-a-something..."

"Fugitives?"

"Aye, them." Suddenly he went stock-still and sat up straight, mouth open.

"Granpa, granpa," he whispered urgently. "I see something..."

"What is it, lad?" Mackie covered the distance to the rock in two strides.

Jamie still sat motionless, gripping the binoculars. "In the water.. it must be her, it must be Nessie!."

"Let me see, lad..."

"Wait...wait..." Quickly, Jamie pointed and handed the glasses to Mackie. "Over there, just before that inlet...it's like...like lumps in the water, one after another... I just know it's her!"

It took Mackie a moment to fix on the black water across the loch. He surveyed both left and right, to try and get a glimpse of what Jamie described. Flashes of sunlight glinted on ripples and waves, then the water gradually smoothed. After several minutes, he lowered the glasses. "It's no good, Jamie lad, I couldna see a thing. Just water." He returned the binoculars to his grandson, who regarded him somberly.

"I really did see something, granpa..."

"...I believe you, lad..."

"...something I never did see before, in all the years I've been here!"

At that, Mackie had to bite his cheek to keep from

laughing, 'all the years' coming as it did from a nine-year-old.

"Let's pack it in, Jamie boy. I didna bring my watch, but I believe it must be time for tea at the pub!"

"Whoosh!" Jamie lept from the rock, clambered up the rocky slope like a Highland goat and was in the car before Mackie had put out his pipe.

Jamie Mackenzie was enchanted. Not by selkies, water-nix, nor fairies, nothing as ethereal; no, he was entranced by the Kilt & Sporran Pub the very first time he and his granpa Mackie went there for tea. From the sign that hung outside, depicting a tall piper bedecked in traditional Scottish regalia, to the massive door with the jangling bell over top, from the long oak bar where the regulars sat at their favorite stools, to the dart board hung high on the far wall: surely no wizard of old ever frequented a more magical establishment. Granma Florrie at first protested Jamie's pub visits but was won over by Mackie's assurance.

"Now dearie, it's just for passing the time...there's na' harm."

Its smell was grand, that of pipe-smoke, potatoes and sausage, freshly-drawn ale, and just a hint of whiskey. Even the sounds were a comfort: the deep rumble of glasses sliding down the bar, the clink of plates and cutlery, coins clattering in the register, occasional singing, laughter, and stories... unending stories. Regulars at the pub drew upon an unexhaustable repertoire of tales about ghosts and goblins, hell-horses, mermaids and seal-people, but the most intriguing of all were of Nessie, fabled denizen of

Loch Ness.

Mr. Culburnie was Jamie's favorite. A youngish man who always wore a tweed cap on his early-balding head, he was the Nessie authority. His job as a locksmith brought him out at all hours, and he claimed to have got a good look at her three times, twice clearly and once just as she submerged into the loch. Culburnie and the rest who had seen her formed a brotherhood of confirmed believers, in unswayable Scots fashion, sticking fast to their claims and damn all skeptics. Jamie hung on their every word.

"Will Mr. Culburnie be there today, d'ye know?" he asked as they neared the village.

"Most probably."

"M' I have a pint of ginger, please, granpa..."

"Aye, lad."

"...and a biscuit, no, a crumpet if they've any, please, may I?" Anticipation was on him like a bee in his bonnet, and he squirmed and bounced on the seat next to Mackie the whole way.

Mackie pulled up at the kerb and set the emergency brake. "You're a pest an' that's the truth." Shaking his head, he ushered Jamie inside the Kilt & Sporran. "On your best behavior, now."

With the door scarcely open, Jamie made straight for the bar, calling, "Davy, Davy, come quick!"

The barman poked his head out of the kitchen, brandishing a towel. "What's all the fuss then?"

"I saw her, I saw her!"

"Saw who?" Davy asked, wiping a clean glass.

"Nessie! In the Loch! I saw Nessie!"

Davy raised his eyebrows and turned inquiringly to Mackie, who responded with eyebrows raised and palms open.

"Ah, are y'sure now?" Davy continued to polish the glass.

"Aye, I'm exactly sure." Jamie nodded, mouth set determinedly. He spied Culburnie at his usual table and ran pell-mell to share the news.

At the bar, Mackie ordered Jamie his ginger ale while Davy prepared the usual pot of tea. "Not a drop o' whiskey for you in some ten-odd years now, Mackenzie."

"Aye, it surprises even myself."

"Did y'get a look at Nessie then?" Davy asked, wiping the bar.

Mackie took a long pull on his tea.

"I didna and that's a fact, but if Jamie says he did, then that's what was and no bones about it." He set his cup down firmly on the polished bar.

At the table with Culburnie, Jamie proceeded to relate every detail of the day's events.

"I saw her with Granpa's field glasses. I was looking to the other shore, that's when I saw her back, sticking up in the water—" Jamie made an up-and-down traveling motion with his hand.

"Was her head sticking up too?" Culburnie asked.

Jamie shook his head. "Only her back. And p'raps might've been her tail- it was this long—" arms stretched wide— "... all bobbing up and down in the water." Culburnie lifted up his tweed cap to scratch his forehead. Cameron and McDougall, other regulars at the pub, pulled up chairs, eager to join in the conversation.

"Ah, 'twas only an old tire, I'll wager."

"Them ripples might a' been a school of fish..."

"You're daft, there's na' been a fish in that loch for ten years on," Culburnie said, leaning back in his chair.

"A motor launch, then..."

"Aye and invisible in the bargain, y'dinna think they'd've seen a boat?"

"There was na' boat, we'd have heard," Jamie chimed in.

Cameron and McDougall conceded and returned amiably to their pints while Jamie finished up his ginger ale.

"Come along, lad, we'd best be getting home," Mackie called from the bar.

"Bye just for now." Culburnie grinned at Jamie. "Been quite the day, I'll wager."

Jamie winked, then turned and skipped to the door as Mackie turned and waved.

Jubilant on the way home, Jamie asked "D'ye think they believed me then?"

Mackie nodded. He recalled the stories of cronies who actually claimed to have seen Loch Ness' elusive occupant. Not the glorified versions that grew more elaborate with each retelling, but the very first report, made with eyes wide, voice subdued, earnest countenance and matter of fact narrative, frequently punctuated with'"I swear to Jesus!" and concluded with a stiff draught of whiskey.

"Aye, lad, yes I do." Jamie scooted over next to his grandfather and sighed contentedly.

# TEN DRAGON TAILS

Once home, Florrie chided gently them at the door. "You missed tea."

"Granma Florrie, I saw Nessie! In the Loch! I saw her!" Jamie ran to grab hold of Glenlivet, Florrie's lethargic cat. He dragged her to a chair in the corner and scratched her chin as Mackie hung up his coat.

"You saw her? And what does she look like then?"

"Humps, great floating humps in the water." As he made the up-and-down motion with his hand again, Glenlivet reached lazily at it with one fat paw. " P'r'aps her tail too. I saw her floating along and then she went back into the loch."

Florrie turned inquiringly to Mackie. "And you?"

"By the time I got the glasses, I couldna see a thing."

Florrie shook her head and laughed. "Well then, try and see the dustbin while you clean the ashes from the stove."

Later that evening, when Jamie was in bed, Florrie pressed for more on the Nessie sighting.

"Jamie's a bit of a bookish lad, Florrie, but you know he's not one to tell lies. No, I saw the look on his face peerin' through them glasses. I know he saw somethin'."

"Lies, now Mackie! I didna say the lad told a lie, I was wanting to know if you had seen..."

"I know, dearie, now. And I wish I had seen her, the great beastie! All I saw today was the sun on the water." He bent low and kissed her pink cheek. "Get along t'bed, I'll bank up the fire and be along in a wee bit."

Florrie yawned. "And put out the cat?"

"Aye."

Alone in the darkened room, Mackie remembered back, ten years before, to the night he hit the goat...
He'd had too many mugfuls to count at the pub, and although Florrie had a few as well, she expressed some concern...

"Can you drive, Mackie?"

"Y've never been in better hands, lassie." Singing and feeling no pain, he had driven back home along the road by the loch. Suddenly the apparition appeared in the middle of the road: an enormous ram, staring stubbornly into the glare of the headlamps. Florrie screamed and grabbed his arm, Mackie laid on the brakes with everything he had, pushing on the horn button and shouting, but it was no good. The car collided with the goat, there was a great crash and a mighty ker-thunk, then the engine coughed and stalled.

"Oh dear, oh dear." Florrie, rubbing her temple, seemed dazed. "What happened?"

Mackie put his arm around her and took her chin in his hand.

"Y've a wee bump on the head, is all. Stay here while I have a look outside."

Spotlighted by a single headlamp, the goat lay dead in front of the car.

Mackie was well acquainted with it. It was notorious for standing at the crossroads, ramming lorries that stopped, and chasing passing bicyclists. The locals called it the Antichrist. But never mind that it had been an ill tempered, obstinate beast; now it lay dead as a wedge in the middle of the road.

"What is it, Mackie?" Florrie called, her voice quivering.

"Ah...It appears we've hit a goat..."

"Is it..."

"I'm afraid there's nothing to be done..."

Florrie burst into tears. She had a soft spot for any living creature, no matter how cantankerous, and seeing one killed sent her straight over the edge. Aye, Mackie told himself as his boots crunched on the glass of the broken headlamp, it was going to be a long night.

Back in the car, he comforted Florrie as best he could on the way home and at last her sobbing subsided.

"Mackie?"

"Yes, Florrie dear."

"I'm never goin' to drink again."

"All right, dear," Mackie replied, reflecting that Florrie drank perhaps twice a year, if that.

"'Promise me one thing."

"Aye?"

"That you'll never take another drink..."

"Well now, I don't see..." Mackie balked at such a harsh penance. Damn that abominable goat!

"What if it had been a wee child there in the road," Florrie protested, sniffing.

"But.." Surely the woman would listen to reason.

"Please, Mackie, you've got to promise." His head thrashing, stomach churning, and what with the car heater having suffered some damage in the collision, feeling quite cold to the bone, Mackie was worn down.

"I swear, Florrie. " With that she commenced crying

all over again.

Never was Mackie as glad to get home. Once inside, he made Florrie an ice compress for her head and a pot of hot tea.

"Mackie-"

"Yes?" he answered reluctantly, fearing further deprivation.

"'Twould be a Christian thing to do, to take that poor animal off the road and bury it."

"Can it not wait 'till morning?" Having taken the Pledge, Mackie drew the line at going back out in the cold dark to perform a funeral for a goat.

"Well I suppose..." Grateful, he put her to bed with a hot water bottle. Good as his word, Mackie was up next morning at dawn and ventured out to find the day foggy and foreboding. Although familiar with the road, he retraced the journey slowly, half because of limited visibility, half because of his hangover.

He found the exact place by the broken glass from the headlamp. Mackie pulled over and set the brake, got out and looked round for the dead animal. He paced up, down, over and back again. There was no goat. As he opened the car door, he glanced down and saw a dark stain on the tarmac. He bent down closer: it was a pool of drying blood and, leading from it, smeared drops and streaks. Mackie's head began to pound as he followed the trail, across the road, down the slope, and across the beach. He traced it to the water's edge, and stopped, puzzled. Then he heard the sound, coming from the loch: a hoarse bellow it was, out of the fog and mist, like a long, drawn-out seal-bark call, once, twice, a pause, then once more.

"Jesus Almighty Christ!" Teeth chattering, head spinning, hands shaking, Mackie ran for the car, nearly slipping on the damp roadway. Tires screeching, he turned right round in the road and sped along back home.

He'd made pot of tea, the consistency of road tar, and drank it all before Florrie was up. He'd assured her that everything was taken care of, but told her nothing about the events of the morning. Further, good to his word, Mackie had not taken a drop of liquor from that day.

Andrew Mackenzie believed there was something in Loch Ness, all right. Even so, although he savored sharing tales with his mates at the pub, he preferred to keep his own encounter to himself.

The following Thursday morning, Florrie announced her committee was arriving shortly for a church bazaar meeting. The motivation to escape a houseful of chattering Episcopalian women was sufficient; Mackie and Jamie packed a picnic basket and a flask full of hot tea.

"Off we go, then, lad. 'From ghosties and ghoulies,'" Mackie intoned,

"'and long-legged beasties'..." Jamie continued,

"...an' parlors full of church ladies, Good Lord deliver us!" Mackie grabbed a handful of ginger biscuits off a plate and Florrie swatted them both with a tea-towel as they fled, laughing, out the kitchen door.

Morning fog hung about like cotton-wool, only damp and cold. Mackie started the car, turned on the heater, and they were off.

"I like the fog, granpa." Jamie rubbed a small circle on his moist window.

"Oh do y', now." Mackie flicked on the windscreen wipers.

"Me an' dad used to go walking sometimes in Edinburgh, evenings, in the fog. I think it's magical, as if there's a great cloud sailing you along, with flying creatures, all in white..."

"Birds?"

"No, griffins! An' flying horses an' unicorns..."

"Unicorns fly?"

"Aye." Jamie nodded. "I've pictures in a book."

Mackie smiled. "It must be a grand book then."

"I'll lend it you, if you like!"

The fog began to thin into long wisps. At last able to get his bearings, Mackie pulled off the road.

"Where are we?"

"At the usual spot."

"Looks different."

"It's your magical fog, lad." Visibility was sorely limited, so provisions were brought out. Just as the biscuits were finished off, the fog lifted and pale lemon-colored sunlight flashed on ripples of water. The pair hiked down to the beach, toward the smell of damp earth and brackish water. Jamie took up a position on his familiar rock, slippery with moisture.

"D'ye hear the birds, Granpa?"

"Aye, crows prob'ly." As Mackie shrugged deeper into his overcoat, he heard a distant splashing.

"Can you see?" Jamie asked from his perch.

"Not to the other shore..."

"I'll fetch the glasses!" Jamie scampered off.

"Mind yer footing now!" Slowly and deliberatly, Mackie made his way up to the high rock and listened.

There it was again: the splashing. Then, despite his heavy coat, Mackie was chilled right to his heart. The call, like a drawn-out seal-bark, came from across the loch. Kneeling down, not even moving to draw a breath, Mackie waited, listening.

"Ke-raw! Ke-raw! Ke-raw! " Startled, he nearly lost his balance as three crows swept raucously overhead in the high grey mist. "Cursed bloody crows," he said aloud, jamming his cold hands into his pockets and wishing he'd brought the dewar flask of tea.

Jamie returned with the binoculars.

"Have a look, lad, and see what ye can make out."

Jamie scanned the water as far as visible, just making out the opposite shore. Ripples made small waves on the beach below. Then they grew bigger and bigger, faster and faster, splashing up onto the rocks...

"Give over the glasses, lad." Mackie put the binoculars to his eyes, trained in on the distant water, on the waves and ripples as they parted. Then from their center a shape bobbed to the surface. At first Mackie thought it was a short log, floating in the loch, but instead of floating it came up entirely out of the water. Not a log, it was a head, horse-like but narrowed about the mouth with what looked like two sets of ears. No sooner did Mackie take in that sight, but the head continued to rise out of the water, up, up, on an elongated, sleek neck. His heart began to pound and underneath his overcoat he could feel hairs on his arms tingling.

"Almighty Jesus Christ!" Mackie whispered. Jamie was at once at his side, arm around his grandfather's shoulders, as much for comfort as curiosity.

"Whatisit, whatisit, whatisit?" he whispered straight into Mackie's ear.

"Shhhhhh." Mackie kept the glasses trained on the beast, as it turned, and for a split second appeared to look straight at them. As the creature moved, part of its back emerged from the water, a dark gray-green, glistening wet. Mackie kept the glasses in same position and moved Jamie in for a look. "Here lad, dinna make a sound..." With a steadying hand on his grandson's shoulder, he suddenly felt the boy stiffen, heard a quick intake of breath.

"D'ye see her, lad.."

"Aye..." Jamie answered in slow amazement, then suddenly flattened himself on the rock, hissing urgently and grabbing Mackie's coat.

"Granpa, get down, she'll see us!"

"OOF!" Mackie belly-flopped onto the cold rock. They both lay prone for what seemed an eternity, motionless, silently watching as the creature dove and surfaced, rolling like a gigantic otter in the loch. At length, Mackie glanced down and noticed his hand casting a shadow. He tugged at Jamie's sleeve.

"The high fog's burning off above, lad. We'd best get off this rock or she'll see us." Jamie nodded wordlessly, lips pursed, cheeks pink with cold. They eased down, behind two smaller sloping boulders forming a 'v'. There, crouched hidden behind rocks, they had a prime view what was, most certainly and without doubt, the Loch Ness Monster.

Jamie and his grandfather took turns with the binoculars and reported details. "Look, she's got two pair of ears." "No...it's not ears, they're small horns atop her head." "See the great fins, up on her back." Her elegant head lifted way up, as she again made her seal-bark. "She's calling out!" Then she submerged with a splash.

"She's gone..." Dejected, Jamie handed the glasses to Mackie. As he took a deep disappointed breath, a wild goose flew over and landed. It paddled about for a moment, then with a furious flash of feathers and a garbled squawk, sharp jaws like scissors flew straight out of the water and clamped down on the bird.

"Granpa! She's caught the goose!" Jamie whispered excitedly.

"Aye..."

A red stain spread over its feathers as the goose ceased moving. Majestically Nessie made her way to shore and came out of the water.

"It's your Nessie, lad."

"Oh, my..."

"D'ye see the size of her!"

"It's Nessie, hooray, hooray!" Jamie hugged himself in quiet glee, then he and Mackie frantically traded the fieldglasses to and fro, vying for a look.

She walked on all fours, two smaller legs in front and two larger, more muscular at rear. A ridge, like a massive dorsal fin, trailed down her back and all along her tail. She was mostly a dark grey-green, but as she turned, a lighter shade of green was visible on her underside, yellowish and striped, like a turtle. She made her way up the pebbly beach, then settled down and in dainty fashion, held her catch with smaller front claws as she tore off small portions.

"Look, lad, at her talons, like a bird's," Mackie urged softly. Jamie nodded, spellbound as Nessie flipped a morsel into the air, extended her neck, caught it neatly and gulped it down.

"Playin' with her food," he nudged Mackie, grinning.

Her meal finished, she climbed slowly up to a high flat rock formation. Once again she extended her long neck, head turning this way and that, flexing in the pale afternoon sunlight. Then as Jamie trained in the glasses for an even better look, what they had taken for fins raised up and outward on each side, farther and farther, taut and supple, the warm brown-grey color of a seal pup.

Nessie spread out her vast wings and flapped them smartly. Mackie and Jamie could hear the *whap, whap* even across the loch.

"Did you see..."

"Almighty Jesus Christ!..."

"Oh m' God...Granpa... Nessie is a dragon!"

"Aye...aye, she is, and a grand beastie!" For long, precious minutes, they took in her every movement: the lazy way her tail coiled around her side, her pinkish tongue curling out as she yawned, her head bending low so she could scratch behind one ear, further flexing of her wings. Then she made her way to the outermost edge of rock, extended her wings, and pushed off. Downward she sailed, her wings billowing like the sails on a longship, then she glided round and flapped off, into the distant foggy stretch of the loch. Jamie and his grandfather watched, with the glasses, until Nessie was only a speck, until even that disappeared.

The pair sat wordless, looking at one another, open-mouthed, united in amazement.

"D'ye believe it, lad?" Mackie said at last, very softly, even though Nessie was no longer there.

"Isn't she grand!" Jamie replied, still staring out into the distant grayness, shaking his head. Then in a hopeful tone, "D'ye'think, will she come back?"

"We'll wait a bit now..." Fog and damp began to creep around them. "Dinna think she'll be back today, lad." Mackie stood up, stiff and cold. His arse was numb and his other extremities were not to be trusted. "Gie' us a hand there, Jamie..." Wordlessly, arm in arm, the pair made their way back to car.

With one more long look out at the still, black water, Mackie started the engine.

"To the pub, then?"

Jamie nodded, bouncing and rubbing his hands together with delight. "I canna wait to tell Culburnie!"

As the car pulled alongside the kerb at the pub, Jamie noticed something unusual. "Look at the odd car, Granpa."

"Strange little thing, English prob'ly."

"But whose is it?"

"Dinna ken, lad. Come along now, you're cold as a corpse. It's a pot of tea for us both right now." As Mackie pulled open the door, warmth and noise wrapped round them like a tartan and drew them in.

The pub was packed, unusual for a weekday, and the only booth available was at the far end across from kitchen.

"It's bedlam today," Mackie spoke down into Jamie's ear and the boy nodded. The din centered around a booth near the bar, where one loud voice carried on.

"Hell, you guys couldn't even count all the krauts me and my squad blew up. I ain't kiddin', between shootin' the bastards from the air and droppin' bombs on 'em, my squad just about beat Hitler single-handed. Just like shootin' fish in a barrel..."

Jamie craned his neck around the side of the booth, eyes wide. The regulars at the Kilt & Sporran sat spellbound at a table covered with empty beer glasses. The object of their awe: a stocky, square-jawed young man, blond hair, shirtsleeves rolled up, cigarette hanging from corner of his mouth.

"Hey pal, what does a guy hafta do to get a refill in this joint?" the stranger called out to Davy at the bar. Passing by their table with a full pint, Davy leaned over and explained "Got a visiting Yank pilot, on leave.'"

Mackie motioned at Davy, on his way back to the bar.

"What'll it be today?"

"Two pots o' tea and scotch eggs, if you'd be so kind." Davy nodded and disappeared into the kitchen. Mackie and Jamie listened in once again.

"'....so whaddya do for excitement around here?"

"Darts..."

"Rugby."

"What the hell's rugby?"

"It's a bit like soccer..."

"Jeez! Doncha do anything normal? Ya ever do any hunting?"

"Oh, aye."

"Well?"

"Pheasant, grouse, bit o' rabbit..."

"Come on, pal, that ain't nothing. Ya got any elk? Buffalo? Bears? Jeez, a good thing you guys weren't in the army, much as you know about hunting! Ya do any fishin' around here?"

"Aye, in the streams.."

"Aw, hell. Aint'cha got no lakes where a man can really catch something?"

"Tell him t'go by Loch Ness," MacDougall shouted.

Mackie sat up rigid. Jamie stared across at him, eyes wide.

Culburnie laughed and slapped the table. "Oh aye laddie, we've got the fish for you."

"Well lemme in on it, that's more like it!" The American in turn pounded the table, making the glasses jump and clink.

Culburnie leaned toward the American and lowered his voice, as though conveying a secret. "'D' ye ever hear o' the Loch Ness Monster?'"

Jamie grabbed across the table at Mackie's hand.

"Monster? That don't sound like no fish to me, pal. What is this thing?"

"Well, we can't tell exactly..."

"...some have seen her..."

"...and some think they've seen her..."

"...there's the photographs..."

"...aye..."

"...she lives in the loch..."

"Lock?"

"Lake, you Yanks would call it."

"How big is it?"

"Wha', the Loch?"

"Naw, this fish-monster!"

"That would be hard to tell, she's na' been seen outside the water."

"She? Whaddya mean 'she,' how do ya know it ain't a 'he'?"

"Truth is, we don't know. We just call her Nessie."

Mackie and Jamie sat listening, still as stones.

"Well then pal, say, what's your name?"

"Culburnie."

"...okay, Burnie, whaddya say you show me how to get t' this Lock Nest so's I can take a look at your monster?"

Culburnie commenced drawing a map on a piece of newspaper while the visitor talked away. "Tell you what, I done some deep-sea fishin' off the coast of Florida before the war. I been all the way to Bah-Jah California. Bet ya never even heard o' those places..." Culburnie glanced up, then continued mapping. "Tell you one thing, pal- you don't just take your fishin' pole to bring in the big ones, no siree bob. You pack along a rifle and once that sucker is hooked, you let him have it. Blam!"

Listening in the booth, Jamie jumped and gasped.

Mackie motioned across the table and mouthed *shhhh*. The crowd had grown more quiet. Culburnie indicated the route traced on the map. "It's sure the right place when you see Urquhardt Castle across the water..."

"Urk-Wart? Sounds like a frog. You Scotch give things the dumbest names I ever heard."

Culburnie paused and sat back, crossing his arms. He was quiet a moment, then added, "If the fog is heavy, count three miles from the crossroads." He gestured at the map.

"When should I go out there, anyway?"

Picking up a tray of empty glasses, Davy chimed in. "Arrive at first light, so y'can be there all the day. Y'would na' want to miss her, now..."

"Yeah, I'll say. Well, I'll be ready. Got my GI pistol in my duffel bag. Yes sir, just might be takin' home a mighty big trophy. A monster's better'n a moose any old day!" He stood up, tossed a handful of coins on the table, and gave Culburnie a mock-salute."Thanks for the tip, sport. Be seein' ya!"

Flipping a brown leather jacket over his shoulder, the young man opened the door. The bell jangled as it banged shut behind him; for a moment the Kilt & Sporran was quiet, then erupted in laughter.

"Full of himself, that one is—"

"Aye.."

"Regular cock o' the walk."

"If all Yanks are bloody fools the like o' him, it's a wonder they won the war," Davy put in, as he brought their tea and eggs.

Mackie poured a cup of tea and held it to warm his

hands. "Are y' not telling what we saw?"

Jamie shook his head anxiously.""There's no time, Granpa. We have to do something!" Ignoring his food, he took hold of Mackie's hand. "I don't want that horrid man to get Nessie, he'll kill her and stuff her and take her back to America, please, granpa, we have to do something!"

Mackie squeezed his grandson's shoulder comfortingly. He doubted anyone, even a braggart Yank, could manage the capture of Nessie. But armed with a pistol...

"Dinna ken wha' we'll do, lad. But we'll go out to the loch..."

"..We can warn her!" Jamie squeezed his grandfather's hand excitedly.

"...tomorrow, early. We know the way better than most..."

"We can save her, oh granpa, thank you, thank you..."

Mackie took both Jamie's hands in his and gave a firm nod. "Right, then. Eat now, lad." Both ate in silence for several minutes until Mackie looked up again.

"And best not be telling your Gram..." As he finished his eggs, Jamie nodded in solemn agreement.

Home again, Florrie gave them a warm welcome. "About time you were back! All the ladies asked about you."

"What ladies?"Jamie asked absently.

"The bazaar committee, of course!"

Mackie and Jamie exchanged wide-eyed glances, having completely forgot. "Oh, of course, and it came off well then?" asked Mackie, quick to recover.

"Oh, yes..."

"Good. And by the way, we're leaving for fishing in the morning, before dawn."

"So early!"

"We're going to try a new place..."

"You're both daft." Florrie shook her head.""There's still some biscuits on the sideboard. Be sure an' brew up a pot of tea."

"Thank you, dearie."

"Well, fetch your dearie a bit of firewood, there's a good man." Mackie and Jamie winked at each other as they headed out for the woodpile.

Mackie rose when the alarm sounded and let Florrie sleep. He dressed quickly and opened the bedroom door, to see his co-conspirator ready and waiting for him, holding the biscuit tin.

"H'mm." Mackie ruffled Jamie's hair. "It's a pot of tea in the flask, then we're off." Provisions ready, they ventured out to the car. Fog hung thickly and a slick mist lay everywhere.

Just like the morning he went back for the goat... Mackie's stomach dropped like a stone.

They drove along in silence as Mackie navigated the road by heart, aided by occasional glimpses through the fog. Just beyond the crossroads, a shape loomed up and he laid on the brakes.

"Hiy!" Jamie blurted out, bracing himself on the dashboard. "What is it, granpa?"

Mackie set the brake and opened his door. Jamie rolled down his window and they both peered out into the gray.

"Granpa, I think it's that funny automobile what was at the pub!"

"Aye." Mackie nodded slowly. "Likely it was sub-let to the Yank."

"Can we have a look then?" Jamie's door was half-open already.

"Slow, now." The two Mackenzies advanced on the car cautiously.

"Wha'...!" Startled, Mackie nearly tripped over something in the road. It clattered to a stop just by a front tire.

Jamie bent down, then burst out, "It's a gun!"

"Hold up, lad. Dinna touch it. Best leave it be." Mackie stooped lower to get a look at the firearm and found himself face to face with his grandson, eyes brimming with tears.

"..d'ye think....has he killed her?"

Mackie frowned. For once in his life he was at a loss for words. Fortunately none proved necessary, for next moment, from the loch came a distant splashing, followed by several long seal-barks. Mackie straightened up at once and seized Jamie's hand.

"D'ye nae hear her, lad, there's your beastie, safe and sound now!" Jamie hugged his grandfather's waist and laughed through tears of relief.

"...and he canna' hurt her, he's nae got his gun!" he added jubilantly.

"The fog's too thick to see just now, Jamie lad. Let's

nip back to the car while we wait a bit."

"...and have some tea and biscuits!"

"Aye."

They passed the cup of scalding tea back and forth, the biscuit tin between them. Soon the windows steamed up and Jamie made a long squiggly line, then added feet, a head, and wings. "Look, Granpa."

"Why, it's Nessie to be sure. A fine likeness."

Jamie looked at it for a long moment, then carefully and deliberately wiped the window clean with his coatsleeve. "D'ye think...will she be all right?"

"Appears to me she can take care of herself. I wouldna' worry." Mackie tucked his arm around his grandson's shoulders. "She's a magical creature, out there in the magical fog."

The fog became lighter, as the pale sun broke through. Jamie rolled down his window. "I want to hear her if she calls," he explained, resting his chin on the window edge. "I've been thinking..." he began seriously. "If we let on, then more like ...like *him* will want to come. I don't want anyone to harm her. Can we... let's... just have it our secret?"

"Aye Jamie. That it will be." Mackie sighed. "O'course, even if we let on, most would think we're daft in the bargain..."

"...except Culburnie..."

"...and there's times I think *he's* daft..."

Jamie turned to Mackie in amazement, then began to giggle. Mackie chuckled at his own joke, then began to laugh harder. Jamie was convulsed with humor and soon both were crying tears of mirth. Mackie put the top on the flask and started the car up. Jamie put his head out the window and waved.

"Bye, Nessie! Bye for now!" The sun shone brightly all the way home.

As they arrived, Florrie met them at the door, hands waving excitedly.

"Ring up Culburnie now, he's just called from the pub, all wrought up." Mackie and Jamie exchanged glances, then Mackie went to the telephone.

"Davy? Andrew MacKenzie here, is Culburnie about?...Culburnie? Florrie said you rang up?...Aye...when?" The question came so sharply that Jamie stopped, rooted to the spot.

"Where?...What did he...aye...ah...oh, my...do tell, now...well, that's best then...aye...well, bye for now, then." Florrie and Jamie stood in the kitchen doorway, oozing curiosity.

"Well, don't keep us in suspense, man!" Florrie began. Jamie chewed his left thumbnail, a look of dread on his face.

"Well, it seems a young man on leave from the American army came wanderin' into the pub this afternoon, cold, wet and ranting on and on, claimed he'd seen something out near the loch...apparently he'd been out there a good part of the night..."

"Och, the poor young man, he could be taken with a fever..."

"...taken a wee dram too many, more's likely." Mackie

retorted. "At any rate, he's to be shipped home tomorrow, so all's well that..."

"What did he see, Granpa, what?" Jamie blurted out.

"According to Culburnie, some great beast with wings an' all, prob'ly breathing fire and carrying off sheep..." The look on Jamie's face passed from amazement to relief.

Florrie was ever-charitable.. "He may have gone daft from the war..." at this Mackie and Jamie began to snicker. "Now, it's a shame and you know it. Ah, my." She filled the teakettle and got out bread and butter. "And now, how was luck at the new fishing place?"

"Oh, it was very lucky, Gram," Jamie answered enthusiastically, as he set the jam-pot on the table.

"Aye, dearie," Mackie added, with a wink at his grandson. "We had a big one, but we didna' catch her. She got clean away."

∧∧∧